Mark practised in major commercial law firms for thirty years, specialising in property dispute resolution. He has acted for businesses large and small, including FTSE-listed property companies and household-name corporate occupiers, across the whole range of property-related issues. He has advised upon forfeiture, and pursued or defended possession proceedings, on countless occasions.

He is now a full-time commercial property management law trainer, putting his expertise and experience to good use in training both lawyers and surveyors. He delivers training for providers including MBL Seminars, Central Law Training, Professional Conferences, CPT Events and Solicitors Group.

Mark is also the author of The Lease Guide website (www.theleaseguide.co.uk), which aims to provide helpful and practical guidance in an understandable and digestible format to small businesses taking a lease.

A Practical Guide to Forfeiture of Leases

A Practical Guide to Forfeiture of Leases

Mark Shelton
MA (Hons) Law (Cantab), Non-Practising Solicitor
Commercial Property Management Law Trainer
Author of The Lease Guide website
www.marksheltontraining.co.uk
www.theleaseguide.co.uk

Law Brief Publishing

Published 2020 by Law Brief Publishing, an imprint of Law Brief Publishing Ltd
30 The Parks
Minehead
Somerset
TA24 8BT

www.lawbriefpublishing.com

Paperback: 978-1-911035-93-0

To Sarah, with love and gratitude.

PREFACE

The essence of forfeiture of leases is very simple. A landlord leases a property to a tenant; if the tenant does not perform its side of the bargain by paying the rent and complying with its other obligations in the lease, then the landlord can take the property back.

As regards residential leases, the process is highly restricted, and largely confined in practice to leases over 21 years in length. Agricultural property is routinely let on periodic tenancies, where a landlord's right to terminate does not rely upon some default by the tenant, but is instead usually exercised by a simple notice to quit. It is in relation to commercial leases, therefore, that forfeiture has most relevance, and that will be the focus of this book.

Though the idea of forfeiture may be simple, in practice the law is anything but. Leases, and forfeiture of leases, have been features of English law for centuries, so that the applicable law may be found in a multitude of sometimes archaic cases, and also in a variety of statutory interventions over the years. As a body of law it is sprawling, not always apparently logical, and sometimes absurd and inconvenient in application. It has been judicially described as a minefield.

Among the potential complications is that the landlord's right to forfeit the lease can very easily and inadvertently be lost by 'waiver', and the precautions required to prevent this happening are not only awkward to implement in practice, but also by their nature make it unnecessarily difficult to resolve matters amicably.

Another obstacle to the landlord taking the property back is the law's requirement that (in effect) the punishment must fit the crime. The tenant may quite readily obtain 'relief from forfeiture', restoring it to possession of the property, so long as it adequately remedies any breaches of its obligations. That is reasonable enough, but the applicable law and procedures relating to relief from forfeiture are Byzantine.

For these and other reasons, forfeiture is highly technical, and can be unpredictable, and a landlord who elects to forfeit a lease may not get the outcome it wants at the end of the process. If the object was to recover possession, that may be thwarted by a grant of relief. If the object was just to have any breaches of the tenant's obligations put right, the landlord may find itself with a vacant property on its hands, and the breaches still not addressed.

Why, then, do landlords still make use of forfeiture? First, the idea that if the tenant does not perform the landlord can take the property back continues to make excellent sense to the property-owner. Secondly, if used in the right circumstances, with an awareness of the pitfalls, forfeiture can often be quicker, cheaper and more effective than any other remedy for breach of tenant's obligations.

One day, the Law Commission's admirable proposals to replace the existing law with a new statutory scheme will be implemented. Until then, those who need to venture into the minefield will continue to need guidance such as that attempted by this book.

The law is stated as at 31 January 2020.

Mark Shelton
February 2020

ACKNOWLEDGEMENTS

I am most grateful to Andrew Williams of Exchange Chambers, who volunteered to read this book in draft, and whose comments and suggestions have improved it greatly. Any remaining errors, omissions or infelicities are of course entirely mine.

CONTENTS

CHAPTER ONE
FORFEITURE OF LEASES – OVERVIEW

This chapter describes the law of forfeiture of leases in outline, summarising its main features.

In reading this book, it will be helpful to have a clear idea of the basics of the law of forfeiture, and some of its main features. We begin, therefore, by outlining forfeiture of leases in broad terms. This chapter is a summary and therefore necessarily a simplification to some extent. Fuller discussion of the matters summarised here follows in subsequent chapters.

Nature of forfeiture

Forfeiture simply means termination of the lease by the landlord, for some default by the tenant. Generally, this right is only available to the landlord if the lease expressly so provides. Most commercial leases will contain forfeiture clauses in more or less standard terms, entitling the landlord to forfeit (a) where arrears have been outstanding for a specified, short 'grace period', (b) where the tenant is in breach of any other covenant in the lease, and (c) where the tenant has become insolvent.

Although that is a simple enough idea, the accreted caselaw and legislation concerning forfeiture has complicated matters considerably. The Law Commission has observed of the law of forfeiture that "*it is complex, it lacks coherence, and it can lead to injustice*". The Commission's draft *Landlord and Tenant (Termination of Tenancies) Bill* was first published in 1994, and republished with some changes after a further consultation in 2006. It proposes abolishing the law of forfeiture completely, to replace it with a new statutory scheme. Several of the problems with the existing law will be apparent from this brief overview.

Waiver of the right to forfeit

Where a landlord has a right to forfeit, it follows that it is for the landlord to decide whether or not to exercise it. That decision involves many commercial factors, and circumstances may sometimes point away from forfeiture. On the other hand, it can be a very valuable property right. The landlord may be able to market the property advantageously if it can recover possession from the tenant, or may count on forfeiture as the most effective way of persuading the tenant to put right whatever breach of covenant it has committed.

One of the most problematic aspects of the current law is that this valuable right may easily and inadvertently be lost, or 'waived', by the conduct of the landlord or its agents. Any conduct which acknowledges the continuing existence of the lease (such as continuing to demand rent) will be treated as a choice to allow it to continue, and will amount to a waiver. The first priority for the landlord, therefore, upon realising that it has a right to forfeit, is to ensure that all those dealing with the tenant on its behalf understand that they should do nothing which may amount to a waiver.

The risk of waiver ends when the landlord proceeds to forfeit the lease, since once the right has been exercised it can no longer be waived. Equally the risk ceases to be a concern once the landlord takes a firm and settled decision not to forfeit.

The law makes a distinction, as regards waiver, between breaches of covenant which are considered to be 'continuing', and those which are 'once-and-for-all'. If for example a tenant assigns the lease to a third party without the required consent from the landlord, that is a completed 'once-and-for-all' breach as soon as the assignment has been completed. If the landlord waives its right to forfeit in relation to that breach, then it is gone for all time. By contrast, a right to forfeit arising from a continuing breach of covenant (such as a failure to keep in repair) may be waived, but because of the continuing nature of the breach a fresh right to forfeit arises immediately. Waiver is therefore less of a concern in relation to continuing breaches, but a cautious landlord will still try to avoid it.

In practical terms, avoiding waiver means putting a stop on the rent account, and avoiding any discussions or correspondence with the tenant until such time as either forfeiture has been effected or the landlord has taken a firm decision not to forfeit. The risk of waiver thus distorts or prevents dialogue between landlord and tenant, and stands in the way of sensible negotiated resolutions to disputes.

Section 146 notice

Assuming that the landlord avoids waiving the right, and wishes to proceed to forfeiture, there is an important formality which may need to be complied with first, depending upon the nature of the breach of covenant giving rise to the right to forfeit.

If the tenant's breach of covenant is a simple failure to pay rent, there is no requirement for the landlord to give the tenant any warning before forfeiture. This is an instance of the importance which the law has always attached to rent. Forfeiture is often referred to by judges as the ultimate security for the payment of rent.

In the case of other breaches of covenant, the landlord cannot forfeit without first serving on the tenant a warning notice under *s.146, Law of Property Act 1925*. This 's.146 notice' must identify the breach of covenant, require the tenant to remedy it within a reasonable time, require the tenant to pay compensation for the breach, and will warn the tenant that unless it complies the lease will be forfeited.

If the landlord does not follow this procedure correctly, any recovery of possession which follows will be unlawful, and will potentially expose the landlord to a claim for substantial damages, or at least payment of the tenant's legal costs. The landlord must be particularly careful (a) to identify the breach of covenant accurately in the drafting of the notice, and (b) to allow a reasonable time for remedying of the breach to elapse before forfeiting the lease.

What is a reasonable time must always be a question of fact in all the specific circumstances. It may be very short: discontinuing an unlawful use of the premises, for example, may be done very quickly. On the other hand, remedying a breach of covenant which involves the physical condition of the premises, and may require significant works to be carried out, could take months. The landlord will wish to err on the side of caution.

The law makes a distinction between breaches which are capable of being remedied, and breaches which are 'irremediable'. In simple logic, where a breach of covenant is irremediable, the reasonable time which must be allowed to a tenant to remedy the breach should be nil. Even in the case of an irremediable breach, though, the courts have suggested that the landlord should still leave at least two weeks between service of the s.146 notice and the actual forfeiture.

Service of the s.146 notice does not end the risk of waiver, and the landlord must still be careful to avoid this, right up to the point of the actual forfeiture.

Methods of forfeiture

The landlord must also decide what method of forfeiture to employ. In order to forfeit, the general principle is that the landlord must act so as to show an unequivocal intention to end the lease and recover possession. There are conventionally two ways of doing this: (a) serving court proceedings claiming possession; and (b) recovering possession physically, typically by changing the locks. The latter option is known as 'peaceable re-entry'. The choice as to which method to adopt is entirely unfettered (save that circumstances may make it impossible for the landlord to effect a peaceable re-entry without committing one of the criminal offences referred to below).

From the tenant's point of view, while possession proceedings would of course be unwelcome, the real threat is that of peaceable re-entry. It is a draconian measure, and particularly so if the landlord is forfeiting in reliance upon arrears of rent, when no warning need be given. The tenant may be able to obtain an interim injunction requiring the landlord to allow them to resume possession, but this will be expensive and highly disruptive.

There are restrictions on the exercise of peaceable re-entry. It is a criminal offence to recover possession in this way if any part of the property is let as a dwelling, which means that it should only ever be used in relation to completely non-residential premises. It is also a criminal offence, if there is any person present on the premises who is opposed to the landlord recovering possession, to do so by means of violence against the person or property. As a consequence, peaceable re-entry is usually effected at anti-social hours, when the landlord can count on there being nobody present. A further consequence is that the tenant may forestall peaceable re-entry by ensuring that there is a 24-hour presence at the property.

Peaceable re-entry also presents practical complications as regards clearing the property of the tenant's goods in order to re-let, and is therefore an option which requires some careful thought on the landlord's part.

Serving possession proceedings is subject to no such restrictions, though of course it is slower, more expensive, and has less impact upon the tenant than peaceable re-entry. The peculiarity of this method of for-feiture is that the landlord will have made its demonstration of unequivocal intention to terminate the lease once it has served pro-ceedings; at that point, the lease is forfeited. Of course, the ultimate outcome of the proceedings may not be success for the landlord, and this type of forfeiture is therefore of a provisional nature.

The period while proceedings are taking their course towards con-clusion is known as the 'twilight period', and the management of the property during this period is slightly complicated by the fact that the landlord cannot, logically, enforce any lease terms against the tenant. However, the converse is not true: in a defended forfeiture it is usually the tenant's position that there was no right to forfeit, and that therefore the lease has never been forfeited, and so there is no inconsistency in it enforcing the lease terms against the landlord.

Forfeiture and residential leases

The law gives residential tenants greater protection against their landlords than that afforded to commercial tenants, for obvious reasons.

Sections 166-172, Commonhold and Leasehold Reform Act 2002 create a number of protections against forfeiture for tenants holding long residential leases. The net effect, from the landlord's point of view, is to reduce the effectiveness of forfeiture in relation to such leases. In summary:

- Regardless of any contrary provision in the lease, there are notice requirements which must be met before any payment of rent is due;

- There can be no forfeiture for non-payment of a sum less than £350, or which has remained unpaid for less than three years;

- No s.146 notice may be served unless either the tenant has admitted the breach alleged, or it has been determined by a relevant tribunal that there has been such a breach.

Under *s.81, Housing Act 1996*, there can be no forfeiture of any residential lease (not just long ones) for non-payment of service charge, unless either the tenant has admitted liability for the sum claimed, or it has been finally determined by a relevant tribunal that it is due.

As regards assured tenancies under the *Housing Act 1988*, it is provided by *s.5(1)* that a landlord cannot terminate the tenancy other than by obtaining an order for possession under the Act, thus effectively banning forfeiture. Instead the court may make an order for possession if one of the statutory grounds for possession is made out.

As mentioned above, forfeiture cannot be effected by peaceable re-entry in relation to a residential property (*s.2, Protection from Eviction Act 1977*).

For all these reasons, as regards residential tenancies forfeiture is largely confined to long leases (over 21 years), and comparatively little-used. Therefore, the focus of this book is on forfeiture of commercial leases.

Relief from forfeiture

Even where the landlord establishes that it had an undoubted right to forfeit, and has followed all procedures correctly, it may still not recover possession at the end of the day, because of the availability of relief from forfeiture. The courts have always had an inherent equitable jurisdiction to relieve against forfeiture, and this has been modified and supplemented by statute over a period of nearly 300 years. The resulting patchwork of different jurisdictions and procedures is highly technical and not obviously logical, nor is it easy to predict in operation.

Broadly, a tenant whose lease has been forfeited for non-payment of rent benefits from a statutory right to reinstatement of the lease so long as it pays all the arrears, plus interest, plus the landlord's costs, within six months of the forfeiture (that is a simplification of the applicable time limits, but is usually reliable).

Holders of derivative interests granted out of the lease (i.e. sub-tenants, or holders of a mortgage or charge over the lease) may also apply for relief, and will likewise be required to pay all arrears, interest and costs. Relief, if granted to a derivative interest-holder, may take the form of the grant of a new lease, the court having considerable discretion as to its terms.

Where a lease has been forfeited for some other breach of covenant, the rules as to when an application for relief must be made differ according to the method of forfeiture adopted by the landlord. In the case of forfeiture by court proceedings, any application for relief must be made before the landlord has enforced an order for possession. In the case of peaceable re-entry, an application may be made after the forfeiture, but undue delay in doing so may bar relief.

Again, derivative interest-holders may apply, and if successful will obtain an order for the grant of a new lease. The general principle is that in order to obtain relief against forfeiture for a breach of covenant other than non-payment of rent, the applicant must remedy the breach of covenant, and pay all the landlord's costs.

That brings into play again the distinction between remediable and irremediable breaches, since logic would suggest that if a lease has been forfeited for a breach which was irremediable, it follows that relief cannot be granted. However, this is another confused and unsatisfactory aspect of the law.

The older caselaw identifies irremediable breaches largely by reference to whether a covenant is positive or negative in substance: if a covenant requires some positive performance by the tenant, such as repairing the property, then the tenant who is in default can always remedy the breach by performing the obligation. However, that is very far from being a complete statement of the law, and it is apparent that in practice an irremediable breach does not prevent the grant of relief. The modern law takes as its starting-point the practical and sensible position that most breaches are in principle capable of remedy, and that the approach is to assess what harm has been caused by the breach and whether as a practical matter that can be put right.

Despite all this complication and confusion, the picture which emerges clearly from the decided cases is that, as is conventionally said, the courts "*lean against forfeiture*". There is a reluctance to give the landlord the 'windfall' of early recovery of possession when the applicant for relief has taken steps to ensure that the landlord has suffered no real damage as a result of the underlying breach of covenant.

Availability of relief – practical relevance

It has already been mentioned that a tenant may respond to peaceable re-entry by seeking an interim injunction requiring the landlord to re-admit them to possession of the property. This will usually be obtained, but must rest upon the tenant having applied for relief from forfeiture (or perhaps, in cases of extreme urgency, undertaking to do so as soon as possible); the injunction will restore them to possession pending the outcome of the application for relief.

However, the tenant need not wait until forfeiture has taken place to apply for relief; an application may be made following service of a s.146 notice. It is often a useful step for a tenant to apply before forfeiture; the landlord will then be aware that peaceable re-entry would be futile, and it should be possible to persuade it to restrict itself to forfeiture by means of possession proceedings.

Another practical implication of the availability of relief is that the landlord who has forfeited because the tenant was in arrears of rent faces a period of six months or so when it cannot be certain that there will be no successful application for relief from forfeiture. That complicates re-letting, though there are measures the landlord can take to reduce the risk.

The availability of relief is also a factor to be considered in the decision whether to forfeit the lease in the first place. Landlords typically wish to forfeit for one of two reasons: (a) they want to recover possession from the tenant; or (b) they judge that the tenant will resist forfeiture, and will therefore remedy all breaches of covenant in order to obtain relief. Forfeiture undertaken with that motive is simply a means of applying pressure on the tenant to comply with its covenants.

A landlord who forfeits in order to recover possession must be made aware that the availability of relief means that it is far from guaranteed that possession will be obtained. However, a landlord who forfeits in order to secure the tenant's compliance with the lease covenants must equally be made aware that once forfeiture has been effected it is generally irrevocable.

If the landlord has effected forfeiture by peaceable re-entry, the tenant may simply accept the situation, make no application for relief, and leave the landlord with vacant premises (and the breaches of covenant still not remedied). If the landlord has opted to forfeit instead by serving possession proceedings, the tenant is not obliged to defend them, or make any application for relief. The landlord may, of course, withdraw the proceedings, but that will not revive the lease if the right to forfeit was undisputed.

Forfeiture should therefore be undertaken in the understanding that the tenant will probably obtain relief if it remedies the breaches of covenant, but also in the acceptance that it may not apply for relief, and that the outcome may be a vacant property.

The difficulties raised even in this brief summary demonstrate why it is so desirable that the Law Commission's long-standing proposals to rationalise the law (considered in Chapter 12) be acted upon.

Summary

In essence, the main features of the law of forfeiture of leases are:

- The right for a landlord to forfeit a lease arises by express provision in the lease, where the tenant is in default of its lease obligations.

- The right to forfeit can be very valuable, but may easily be lost by operation of the doctrine of 'waiver'.

- Before forfeiting, except for arrears of rent, the landlord must serve a warning 's.146 notice' on the tenant, and allow them a reasonable time to remedy their breach of covenant.

- Forfeiture may be effected simply by changing the locks, or by serving court proceedings claiming possession.

- Forfeiture is highly restricted and little-used in relation to residential leases.

- Tenants, sub-tenants, and those holding a mortgage or charge over the lease may apply for relief from forfeiture, which may be broadly understood as reinstatement of the lease, and this is readily granted so long as the breaches of covenant are remedied.

- A landlord who wishes to recover possession may be frustrated in this by a grant of relief.

- A landlord who forfeits in order to pressure the tenant into complying with its lease obligations may be left with a vacant property, since forfeiture once done is irrevocable.

CHAPTER TWO
WHEN A LEASE MAY BE
FORFEITED

This chapter outlines the limited circumstances in which forfeiture may be effected without any express right to forfeit being provided for in the lease. It goes on to outline the usual content of a forfeiture clause, with an illustrative example, and considers the nature of the right to forfeit, where it exists.

The right to forfeit is a creature of contract, requiring express provision in the lease. It is an unusual lease which does not contain provision for forfeiture, but they are encountered, and where a tenant who holds such a lease fails to pay the rent, or defaults in some other way, that is highly likely to prompt the landlord to look into whether and if so how the lease may be terminated.

Agreements for lease which provide for the grant of a lease "*on the usual covenants*", are occasionally seen, and in the event of dispute this may of course require a court to decide which covenants are 'usual'. For present purposes the question is whether the lease should include provision for termination by forfeiture. The list of covenants considered to be usual in *Hampshire v Wickens (1878) 7 Ch D 555* did not include a forfeiture provision.

What is 'usual', in such a case, is a question of fact to be decided on the basis of the usage at the time. This approach has been confirmed in the more modern case of *Chester v Buckingham Travel Ltd [1981] 1 All ER 386*, and there the judge considered that the lease *should* include a provision for forfeiture in the event of non-payment of rent or breach of any other lease covenant. The case was not concerned with the effect of a contractual 'usual covenants' provision, however, but with objections to a form of lease drafted by conveyancing counsel of the court, so that the question asked of the court was not quite the same. Perhaps few practitioners would argue against the view that in a modern lease a forfeiture provision is entirely usual.

Such agreements are comparatively rare, though, and the question which might more readily be anticipated is whether, in a lease which has been negotiated between the parties but which does not contain a forfeiture clause, one should be implied into it. (*Chester v Buckingham Travel Ltd* also confirmed that the question of what terms are 'usual' is quite distinct from the question of whether certain terms should be implied). It is conventionally considered that in the absence of an express forfeiture provision, one will not be implied (although see *Abidogun v Frolan Health Care Ltd [2001] EWCA Civ 1821*, below).

This might be a question which arises in relation to another rare creature, a purely oral lease. In such a case the express terms will be few, and it is unlikely that a forfeiture provision will be among them. Again, conventional wisdom is that no such term would be implied.

If no forfeiture provision is implied, then a right to terminate on the basis of tenant default could really only arise on the basis of the landlord's acceptance of a repudiation of the lease by the tenant. This possibility is considered below, but is not promising, from the landlord's point of view.

Generally speaking, then, an express provision in the lease is required in order to forfeit. There are, however, two established situations in which forfeiture may follow without one.

Forfeiture without a forfeiture clause

Denial of title

If a tenant, in a formal statement of case in the course of court proceedings, asserts that the landlord and tenant relationship between it and the landlord does not exist, so that its occupation of the property is based on a title inconsistent with that of the landlord, the landlord is entitled to forfeit the lease. This principle is referred to as 'denial of title'. This sounds an archaic concept, and indeed it is. In his judgment in *Warner v Sampson [1959] 1 All ER 20*, Lord Denning's historical survey of the relevant law includes material dating back to 1181. Nevertheless, *W G Clark (Properties) Ltd v Dupre Properties Ltd [1992] 1 All ER 596* and *Abidogun v Frolan Health Care Ltd [2001] EWCA Civ 1821* provide modern examples of the principle in operation (although the outcome of both cases was actually that the lease was held not to have been terminated).

The courts have wavered somewhat as to the conceptual basis of the principle in the modern law, but after *Abidogun* it seems to be a straightforward matter of an implied condition that the tenant will do nothing to prejudice the landlord's title, breach of which gives rise to a right to forfeit. This brings the principle neatly into line with the law of forfeiture generally, so that *s.146, Law of Property Act 1925* applies, and hence relief from forfeiture is available. Also, before taking action to recover possession based upon denial of title, a landlord must serve a s.146 notice, as would be required in the case of forfeiture based upon a provision in the lease. It is likely (*per* Hodson and Ormerod LJJ in *Warner v Sampson*) that having served a s.146 notice the landlord would then need to effect the forfeiture by means of serving a fresh claim form claiming possession, rather than by means of further pleadings or amendment of pleadings in the existing action.

The tenant may retract its denial of title subsequently, but only if the landlord has not yet re-entered, or commenced proceedings for possession, based upon the denial of title; after that it is too late (*Warner v Sampson*; *Abidogun*).

Breach of condition

A lease may also be terminated for breach of condition (*Freeman v Boyle (1788) 2 Ridg Parl Rep 69*). So, for example, a lease of Oak Tree Farmhouse, together with Oak Tree Farm, might be granted "*on condition that Oak Tree Farm and Oak Tree Farmhouse should remain in common occupation*". Should the farm come into separate occupation the condition would be breached, and the lease could be terminated by the landlord, despite there being no applicable provision in any express forfeiture clause (*Doe d. Lockwood v Clarke (1807) 8 East 185*). As in the case of denial of title, a s.146 notice is required before termination for breach of condition.

However, if the lease were instead expressed as being granted to last "*until such time as Oak Tree Farm and Oak Tree Farmhouse should cease to be in common occupation*", that would not be a condition but a limitation, defining the duration of the term. Upon the beginning of separate occupation, the lease would determine automatically.

The straightforward way of giving effect to the landlord's requirement that Oak Tree Farm and Oak Tree Farmhouse should remain in common occupation throughout the lease term would be a tenant's covenant. The alienation covenant will usually prohibit assignment of part, underletting of part, and parting with possession or occupation of part of the premises. Separate occupation of farm and farmhouse would necessarily amount to a breach of such a covenant, in which case termination of the lease by forfeiture would ordinarily be available, in accordance with the terms of the forfeiture clause.

Whether a term of the lease creates a condition or a limitation, or is a covenant, is a matter of construction of the words used (e.g. *Maley v Fearn [1947] 176 LT 203, Shaw v Coffin (1863) 14 CB (NS) 372*).

Other contractual modes of termination

There is some support in caselaw for the possibility of termination of a lease by frustration. In *National Carriers Ltd v Panalpina Northern Ltd [1981] AC 675*, the House of Lords accepted that in principle this was possible, while emphasising that the circumstances in which it might happen would be exceptional (the obliteration of Oak Tree Farm and Farmhouse by a volcanic eruption, perhaps). There was a recent unsuccessful attempt to establish that a lease had been frustrated by the United Kingdom's decision to leave the European Union, in *Canary Wharf (BP4) T1 Ltd v European Medicines Agency [2019] EWHC 335*

(Ch), and it remains the case that there is no recorded instance of a frustration argument succeeding in relation to a lease.

There have, though, been occasional instances of a lease having been held to be terminated by acceptance of a repudiatory breach.

- In *Hussein v Mehlman [1992] 32 EG 59*, a landlord of residential property which was let on an assured shorthold tenancy agreement was in breach of his repairing obligations, and the County Court concluded that that breach amounted to a repudiation of the tenancy agreement. The tenant vacated the property and returned the keys; in so doing, the court concluded, he had accepted the landlord's repudiation of the tenancy agreement, thereby terminating it.

- In *Chartered Trust plc v Davies (1998) 76 P&CR 396*, the Court of Appeal held that the landlord had repudiated the lease by its derogation from grant, and that the lease had been terminated by acceptance of that repudiation. There was no argument as to the applicability of the doctrine of repudiation, however. It was simply accepted, and *Hussein v Mehlman* was not considered.

- Both cases were relied upon in the High Court in *Nynehead Developments Ltd v RH Fibreboard Containers Ltd [1999] 1 EGLR 7*, as authority for the applicability to leases of repudiation and acceptance, although in that case the landlord's conduct did not, on the facts, amount to repudiation.

- In *Reichman v Beveridge [2006] EWCA Civ 1659*, where some doubt was expressed on the proposition, it was noted that there was no Court of Appeal decision in which the question, whether or not the doctrine of repudiation applied to leases, had been fully argued and ruled upon. It was unnecessary to decide the issue in that case.

- Most recently, in *Grange v Quinn [2013] 1 P&CR 18*, it was stated in the Court of Appeal that: "*it is now clear that a lease may be brought to an end by repudiation and acceptance ... In the present case the defendants' conduct in unlawfully and permanently evicting the claimant was a repudiation which necessarily brought the lease to an end without any need for acceptance.*" Again, though, this was without argument on the point, and the decision for the court in that case was the assessment of damages for unlawful eviction, not whether the lease had been terminated, by whatever means.

Apart from *Reichman v Beveridge*, those were all cases relating to actual or alleged repudiation by the landlord, but when discussing alternatives to forfeiture, the question is whether repudiation by the tenant gives rise to potential to terminate the lease. The prime obligation of a tenant under a lease is to pay rent, and non-payment should usually amount to a repudiation of the lease. That was implicitly assumed, at least for the purposes of argument, in *Reichman v Beveridge*, though there was in that case no acceptance of the repudiation by the landlord. Other tenant obligations, such as the covenant to repair, could potentially be considered sufficiently central to the landlord and tenant relationship that breach could be considered a repudiation. Could a landlord terminate a lease, in the event of the tenant breaching a core obligation, by accepting the repudiation?

It appears unlikely that a court would permit a landlord to avoid in this way the available statutory protections for the tenant, principally relief from forfeiture, and indeed the judge in *Hussein v Mehlman* considered that any purported acceptance of repudiation by the landlord would have to be subject to all statutory provisions applicable to forfeiture, and also to the provisions of the forfeiture clause. Echoing that sentiment, in *Abidogun v Frolan Health Care Ltd [2001] EWCA Civ 1821*, Buxton LJ observed:

"*I can well accept the ... point ... that relations between a landlord and his tenant, under a lease, are governed by the ordinary law of contract as well as by the more specific doctrines of the law of landlord and tenant. It does not, however, follow ... that the protection for a tenant, as has been provided by Parliament in s.146, can be avoided by recourse to a purely contractual doctrine such as that of repudiatory breach."*

The court in *W G Clark (Properties) Ltd v Dupre Properties Ltd [1992] 1 All ER 596* regarded the doctrine of denial of title as analogous to repudiation of a contract, but did not suggest any wider applicability of the idea of termination of a lease by repudiation, and also made it clear that in the specific instance of denial of title, termination by the landlord would require more than a simple 'acceptance' : *"the landlord may accept the repudiation by re-entry or by issuing and serving proceedings claiming possession"* (emphasis supplied).

The caselaw on termination of leases by acceptance of repudiatory breach may be said to be developing; for the most part it will be a reliable assumption that the landlord can only forfeit the lease pursuant to an express forfeiture provision, and in accordance with its terms.

Forfeiture in reliance upon a forfeiture clause

Forfeiture clauses are often referred to as 're-entry' clauses, or as 'provisos for re-entry', and they may be drafted in terms of the landlord 're-entering upon the premises', rather than 'forfeiting the lease'. This is just antique terminology. The effect of the provision is the same, as it is in the case of modern, plain English leases which refer simply to a right to terminate. 'Peaceable re-entry', though, has a technical meaning, being one method of forfeiture, and there is usually provision that the landlord may effect forfeiture of the entirety of the lease by re-entry upon part only of the premises.

Forfeiture clauses tend to be in fairly standard form, usually entitling the landlord to forfeit:

- When the tenant has been in arrears for a certain period (usually 7, 14 or 21 days – commonly referred to as a 'grace period')

- If the tenant is in breach of any other tenant's covenant in the lease

- If the tenant (or any guarantor) has entered into an insolvency procedure.

A long lease of a dwelling, which will usually have a significant capital value, and for which the tenant will therefore probably have paid a large premium financed by a mortgage, is unlikely to provide for forfeiture upon the tenant's insolvency, as that will not be acceptable to a lender.

The length of the grace period is not a matter of uniform practice, and needs to be checked in each case. Also, the content of the provisions relating to insolvency will depend upon the state of insolvency law at the time the lease was entered into – for example, the forfeiture clause of a lease pre-dating 1986 will not contain any reference to the possibility of the tenant going into administration, since the procedure was only introduced in that year.

Another variation sometimes seen in older leases is a right to forfeit should the tenant allow distress to be levied on the premises. Levying distress was a centuries-old landlord's remedy under which a landlord might instruct bailiffs to enter the premises and seize and sell tenant's goods in satisfaction of rent arrears. Levying distress would amount to a waiver of the right to forfeit based on the non-payment of rent, so a provision that levying distress should in itself be a forfeiture event was an attempt to get around that problem, allowing the landlord to levy distress while still being able to forfeit subsequently in the event that the distress did not satisfy all the arrears.

Distress for rent was replaced in 2014 by Commercial Rent Arrears Recovery ("CRAR"), so a modern lease will not make reference to levying distress. That said, use of CRAR will waive any right to forfeit in the same way as levying distress would have, and there is no obvious reason why a forfeiture clause should not adopt the same method of getting around the problem, stipulating the use of CRAR, instead of distress, as one of the forfeiture events.

Wider wording is sometimes seen entitling the landlord to forfeit in the event that a judgment is enforced by means of taking control of the tenant's goods.

Bespoke drafting may be encountered to accommodate specific circumstances. Imagine a tenant who has a lease of Unit 19, Anytown Industrial Estate. Unit 20 becomes available, and the tenant agrees terms for a supplementary lease of that unit. The two units are physically joined, though separate, and the landlord agrees that the tenant may carry out alterations to remove the internal wall between the two units, and to conjoin utilities. The landlord will not thereafter wish to be left with vacant possession of only one of the two units, and one of the ways this might be prevented is to provide that the Unit 19 lease may be forfeited for breach of tenant's covenants contained in the Unit 20 lease, and vice versa. The landlord will therefore be able to forfeit both leases together.

A similar solution might be adopted if the tenant had instead negotiated for a reversionary lease of Unit 19, for example a new five-year lease to commence upon expiry of the present one. A landlord intending to forfeit the present lease would not want the same tenant to pop up again upon commencement of the reversionary lease, and so the reversionary lease would be made liable to forfeiture in the event of any breach of the tenant's covenants in the present lease.

Example forfeiture clause

It may be helpful to see an example of what a forfeiture clause might usually look like. This is not intended as a precedent, nor should it be used as such (particularly the content in relation to events of insolvency, where technical detail has been omitted).

> *6. In the event that:*
>
> > *6.1. any instalment of the Rent due under this Lease is unpaid and outstanding for 14 days or more beyond the due date for payment whether or not formally demanded;*

6.2. there is a breach of any of the covenants on the Tenant's part contained in this Lease;

6.3. an Event of Insolvency occurs in relation to the Tenant or the Guarantor

the Landlord shall be entitled to re-enter upon the Premises or upon part of the Premises in the name of the whole upon which this Lease shall terminate forthwith.

'Event of Insolvency' will of course be defined elsewhere in the lease, and (on the basis of current insolvency law) is likely to include:

In the case of an individual:

- any receiver is appointed over the whole or any part of their assets;

- they enter into any arrangement with their creditors in composition or satisfaction of their debts;

- they propose an individual voluntary arrangement;

- an application is made for their bankruptcy; or

- they apply or become subject to either a debt relief order or a debt management plan.

In the case of a company:

- any receiver is appointed over the whole or any part of its assets;

- it proposes a company voluntary arrangement;

- a petition for winding-up is presented against it, or it enters into liquidation other than for the purposes of reconstruction or amalgamation;

- an administrator is appointed in relation to it; or

- it is struck off the register of companies.

There may be further detailed provision in relation to insolvency of partnerships and limited liability partnerships.

Lease voidable, not void

Where a right to forfeit arises, the effect is not to terminate the lease, but to confer on the landlord a right to do so if it chooses. The lease is not void, but instead is voidable at the landlord's option. This is so even though the wording used may suggest otherwise. For example, in *Doe d. Nash v Birch (1836) 1 M&W 402*, the lease provided that failure by the tenant to carry out certain works within three months should render the lease "*null and void*", but the court held that the effect was only to allow the landlord to elect to terminate.

The rationale is that otherwise a tenant could escape its lease commitments by defaulting in performance of its covenants, thereby taking advantage of its own wrong.

Termination by notice to quit after tenant default

Landlords have sometimes attempted to avoid the complications of the law of forfeiture (and in particular the availability of relief from forfeiture) by stipulating that, after any breach of covenant by the tenant, the landlord should be entitled to terminate the tenancy, not by forfeiture, but by notice to quit. In *Richard Clarke & Co Ltd v Widnall [1976] 1 WLR 845*, the Court of Appeal held that service of a notice to quit by the landlord in such a case amounted to the exercise of a right to forfeit, and that accordingly the tenant was in a position to apply for relief from forfeiture.

Business tenancies and security of tenure

Commercial leases will of course generally fall within *Part II, Landlord and Tenant Act 1954*. If a landlord were to serve a notice to quit under a tenant default provision of the type just described, and if that were held to be effective as a notice to quit, and not as a forfeiture, the effect would still not be to terminate the tenancy, if it were one within the 1954 Act. It would continue pursuant to *s.24(1)* of the Act, unless and until terminated in one of the ways provided for in the Act. The same is not true of forfeiture, since *s.24(2)* provides that business tenancies within *Part II* may be terminated, notwithstanding *s.24(1)*, by certain common law methods, including forfeiture. In passing, those specified common law methods of termination do not include frustration, or acceptance of a repudiatory breach, so there is a question mark over the operation of *Part II* in such circumstances.

Summary

While forfeiture of a lease can usually only be effected if there is an express term in the lease entitling the landlord to forfeit, and only in accordance with its terms, there are limited circumstances in which a lease may be forfeited in the absence of any such express right. They are:

- Denial of title – the tenant formally denies that the landlord is its landlord, in the course of court proceedings; and

- Breach of condition – where a lease is granted conditionally upon some event or state of affairs, and the condition is breached.

Otherwise, leases generally entitle a landlord to forfeit if (a) rent remains unpaid beyond a specified, short 'grace period', (b) the tenant is in breach of some other covenant in the lease, or (c) the tenant becomes insolvent.

While there have been attempts to provide otherwise, the effect of a right to forfeit arising is that only the landlord may elect to void the lease.

CHAPTER THREE
THE DECISION WHETHER
TO FORFEIT

This chapter addresses the 'for' and 'against' factors which will influence the decision whether to exercise a right to forfeit, and which should be considered with landlord clients before embarking upon forfeiture.

A landlord who is contemplating forfeiting a lease needs to be aware of the potential pitfalls of the process, as outlined in the overview of the law given in Chapter 1. That awareness will be one of the factors involved when deciding whether or not forfeiture is a useful way of addressing the specific problem. But even if the process were a completely straightforward one, there are several other commercial and practical matters that the landlord needs to take into account.

For

Effectiveness – simple monetary default

Forfeiture can be a very quick, cheap and effective way of enforcing covenants, at least in the case of simple non-payment. The tenant who is in arrears of rent, and arrives at the premises in the morning to find the locks have been changed, has only one way of getting back in, which is to pay the arrears. Forfeiture is sometimes described as the ultimate security for payment of rent, for this reason. It is surprising how often a tenant which appears to be in serious financial difficulties can manage to re-finance and pay the arrears under this kind of extreme pressure.

However, the availability of forfeiture (whether for monetary default or some other breach of covenant) must be considered in the context of the other potential remedies. Commercial Rent Arrears Recovery, injunction/specific performance, statutory demand, county court debt proceedings, and claims for damages all come with their own advantages and disadvantages.

Commercial Rent Arrears Recovery

Distress for rent was a centuries-old procedure under which landlords could send bailiffs into premises to seize and sell goods in payment of rent arrears, without having to go to court first. Commercial Rent Arrears Recovery ("CRAR") entirely replaced the remedy of distress, and the new regime came into force in 2014. The relevant legislation is the *Tribunals Courts and Enforcement Act 2007, Part 3* and *Schedule 12*, and the *Taking Control of Goods Regulations 2013*.

CRAR can only be used to recover rent (not service charge, insurance premiums or other payments due under the lease), but in practice enforcement agents may combine a CRAR notice with a letter in relation to any non-rent items, written in sufficiently formal terms as to prompt the tenant to deal with all outstanding debts together.

CRAR theoretically depends for its effectiveness upon there being sufficient value in tenant's goods on the premises, since (like distress for rent) the procedure ultimately works by the landlord having the ability to seize and sell goods in satisfaction of the rent arrears. In reality, however, CRAR rarely proceeds to this stage; most often the service of the requisite warning notice prompts the tenant to engage with the problem.

Some enforcement agents offer CRAR to landlords as a completely free service, since they make their money through recovery of fees from tenants. A remedy which is quick, costs nothing and which has a high success rate must naturally be attractive.

The inter-relationship between CRAR and forfeiture needs to be considered, however. *Brar v Thirunavukkrasu [2019] EWCA Civ 2032* confirmed that exercising the remedy of CRAR will waive any right to forfeit which exists at the time, so a landlord who plans to recover as much as is available through CRAR, and then forfeit if any arrears remain outstanding, needs to considers its options carefully.

Another consideration is that if CRAR is pursued to the stage of selling the tenant's stock, raw materials, specialist tools and equipment, etc., the result is likely to be to push the tenant into even worse financial problems, and forfeiture may well follow anyway.

Debt proceedings

The landlord may instead simply issue proceedings, usually in the County Court, to recover the sums due. As the County Court small claims limit continues to rise, and ability to recover the legal costs of small claims becomes ever more restricted, this is increasingly something which landlords may do themselves, usually online, without involving lawyers. If the process results in a default judgment then it can be relatively quick and cheap. If the claim is defended, of course, it may become necessary to instruct lawyers, and the proceedings can quickly become uneconomic to pursue.

All usual enforcement methods will be available in relation to any judgment, principally: taking control of goods, charging orders and third-party debt orders. Once the judgment has been obtained, then the debt is indisputable, and there can be no challenge to enforcement (e.g. *Lee v Sommer [2015] EWHC 3889 (Ch)*).

Involvement of mortgagee

Where there is a mortgage or charge over the lease, the lender will not wish its security to be endangered, and landlords may find it a useful short-cut to payment to notify them of any arrears, or other breach of covenant. The mortgagee may pay the arrears, and add the amount, together with any costs, to the mortgage debt. This neatly transfers the problem from the landlord to the mortgagee. A preliminary to this may be obtaining a judgment against the tenant for the debt, and that may be a necessary preliminary anyway where residential leases are concerned (see Chapter 1).

Statutory demand

Another option for the landlord may be to serve a statutory demand. A statutory demand is not strictly speaking a means of debt recovery. It is a preliminary to insolvency proceedings for liquidation in the case of a company (*s.123(1), Insolvency Act 1986*), or bankruptcy in the case of an individual (*s.268(1), Insolvency Act 1986*). The creditor serves a demand in the specified form, and if the debtor fails to pay within 21 days they are deemed to be unable to pay their debts and can be made insolvent. An individual creditor must owe at least £5000 before a statutory demand can be served on them, while the limit is £750 in the case of a company.

Service of a demand, of course, will be understood by the tenant as a threat of insolvency if payment is not made within 21 days, and it can therefore be a very persuasive way of obtaining payment. For some landlords it is their preferred method of debt recovery.

It should be borne in mind, though, that the courts have frequently expressed their disapproval of the statutory demand process being used as a method of debt collection, and regard it as an abuse of the insolvency procedure (*Mann v Goldstein [1968] 1 WLR 1091; Re a Company (no. 0012209 of 1991) [1992] 1 WLR 351*). It should be said that this line of authority has recently been questioned in *Sell Your Car With Us Ltd v Sareen [2019] EWHC 2332 (Ch)*.

In any event, it is clear that a statutory demand is supposed to be served only in relation to an undisputed debt (*Stonegate Securities Ltd v Gregory [1980] Ch 576*). In the case of sums such as service charge, where liability is often disputed, the demand is liable to be set aside by the court. The same applies where the tenant has a right to set-off some other claim against the debt owed to the landlord (*Re Bayoil SA [1999] 1 WLR 147*).

Where a statutory demand is challenged successfully, the outcome may well be not only that the demand is set aside, but also that an adverse costs order is made against the landlord.

The demand may not be challenged, of course, and the tenant may be unable to pay. The landlord is then faced with the decision whether or not to follow it up by applying for the tenant's insolvency, which in turn will give rise to a new right to forfeit the lease (while typically imposing restrictions on the landlord's ability to exercise the right – see Chapter 11).

Other parties liable

Performance of the tenant's obligations may be guaranteed, typically by a parent company, or by a director/shareholder. Former tenants or their guarantors may additionally be liable. In the case of a lease granted before 1 January 1996 (the date when the *Landlord and Tenant (Covenants) Act 1995* came into force), liability may exist at common law, because these parties will usually have assumed contractual liability for the tenant's obligations throughout the term of the lease, no matter whom it might be vested in from time to time. In the case of leases subject to the statutory regime of the 1995 Act, a former tenant may be liable because it has entered into an Authorised Guarantee Agreement ("AGA"), while its guarantor may have entered into a Guarantee of an Authorised Guarantee Agreement ("sub-AGA" or "GAGA").

Where third parties are liable in this way, it may generally be assumed that in the event of tenant default the landlord will take advantage of the fact by claiming against them, rather than forfeiting the lease. For one thing, that was the whole point in taking that form of security. For another, the liability of those parties is predicated upon the existence of the lease and its terms, so that if it is forfeited, the ability to obtain payment from them in future is lost. Specific circumstances may raise other considerations which lead the landlord to opt for forfeiture instead, but the ability to obtain payment from third parties points strongly in the other direction.

Enforcing the terms of the lease against such parties may require debt proceedings or service of statutory demands, in the same way as enforcement against the tenant.

Recourse against sub-tenants

If the property is fully sub-let, an effective and convenient procedure for securing payment of rent is to serve notice on sub-tenants, under *s.81, Tribunals, Courts and Enforcement Act 2007*. The notice requires sub-tenants to pay their rent to the superior landlord, leap-frogging the head-tenant, until such time as the head-tenant's arrears, specified in the notice, have been paid. Successive notices are needed to keep pace with further unpaid rent instalments. Depending upon the timing, this may mean that the head-tenant is perpetually behind by one rental payment, though at least the arrears will not get worse. Where the rent payable under the sub-lease is higher than that under the head-lease, then the rent payable under the head-lease will eventually be brought up-to-date. This is not a long-term solution, but the availability of this procedure may be an argument against forfeiture, at least in the short-to medium-term.

Rent deposit

If the tenant was required to pay a rent deposit upon taking on the lease, then as in the case of a guarantee, the whole point is to give the landlord security in the form of an additional remedy for non-performance. It will be quick and cheap to draw down sums held on deposit rather than forfeit the lease, and this does not have the drawback of immediately worsening the financial pressure on the tenant.

The tenant will invariably be obliged under the rent deposit deed to top up the deposit in the event of any draw-down, but if they are unable to pay the rent, then they will not be able to do that either. It may therefore simply be postponing the inevitable. A well-drawn rent deposit deed will entitle the landlord to draw down from the deposit both before and after a forfeiture, so that the landlord is not required to choose between forfeiture and draw-down, but can do both.

Absence of other effective remedy

For certain types of non-monetary breach, forfeiture may be the only remedy which is effective. A tenant might, for example, assign its lease without obtaining the landlord's prior written consent, in breach of covenant. The landlord might perhaps be prepared to accept the assignee on appropriate terms (provision of an AGA, rent deposit, etc.), but cannot risk negotiating on those matters, since it is almost inevitable that the right to forfeit will thereby be waived. The landlord must forfeit the lease, and then negotiate for the grant of relief. If the assignee is not acceptable on any terms, then the case for forfeiture is even stronger.

The importance of being able to forfeit may be even more apparent in the case of a lease contracted out of the *Landlord and Tenant Act 1954*, where the tenant breaches the terms of the lease by granting a sub-lease within the Act. The fact that the head-lease is contracted-out will not prevent the sub-tenant from having security of tenure. The only sure way to address that is to forfeit the head-lease, so that the sub-lease falls with it.

An alternative possibility in such cases is to seek an injunction to reverse the transaction, following *Hemingway Securities v Dunraven (1996) 71 P&CR 30* and *Crestfort Ltd v Tesco Stores Ltd [2005] 3 EGLR 25*. This has attractions where other factors point away from forfeiture, since an injunction can restore the situation which existed prior to the breach of covenant, while leaving the lease in place. In a difficult letting market, that may be important. On the other hand, an injunction is a discretionary remedy, and the landlord cannot be absolutely sure of obtaining one.

Another type of breach which presents difficulties arises in relation to retail premises, where a tenant is likely to have covenanted to keep the premises open for trade during normal opening hours. In retail developments, the success of the development as a whole, whether a small arcade of shops or a huge shopping centre, depends on attracting shoppers who will spend money. For that, it is important to have a good mix of shops, all open and trading during the usual opening hours. Leases of units within the development are therefore likely to contain a 'keep-open' covenant. That is especially likely in the case of major lettings to 'anchor tenants', typically a major department store or supermarket, whose presence is essential to attract both shoppers and other, smaller businesses.

Co-operative Insurance Society Ltd v Argyll Stores (Holdings) Ltd [1998] AC 1 concerned just such a tenant (Safeway), which was trading at a loss from a store and decided to close it, in breach of covenant. The landlord sought specific performance, effectively an injunction to compel it to keep the store open. The court refused, on the basis of the need to define with sufficient precision what a defendant must do in order to comply with a mandatory order of this sort. The sanctions for non-compliance are criminal in nature: committal to prison, a fine, or sequestration of assets. The court is therefore very properly concerned that a defendant should be left in no doubt as to what it must do to comply. If an injunction were granted to enforce a keep-open covenant, could the tenant comply by opening only the tobacconist counter, for example? Or by trading with a skeleton staff and a reduced range of goods, and undertaking no promotion of the store? The likely result would be repeated applications to court for future guidance, which the court considered to be an unacceptable basis for a commercial enterprise, as well as putting the court into a supervisory role for which it was unsuited.

Since injunctions will not be granted to enforce keep-open covenants, the question naturally arises what damages are recoverable. *Transworld Land Co v J Sainsbury plc [1990] 2 EGLR 255* is a good example of a landlord successfully claiming substantial damages for breach of a keep-open covenant. The landlord was able to show the impact on its shopping centre of the closure of the Sainsbury's store:

• Reduced footfall;

• Impaired trading performance of other tenants;

- Insolvency or closure of other tenants, resulting in rent voids and under-recovery of service expenditure, insurance premiums etc;

- Reduced rental levels upon rent reviews; and

- Inability to attract new tenants to the centre.

This suggests that in practice it may be more likely that loss can be identified and quantified as against an anchor tenant, or major multiple retailer, than against smaller businesses.

As against the majority of tenants, therefore, the keep-open covenant is really only enforceable by forfeiture. It will often be an unattractive course for the landlord, which would rather have the tenant open and trading, but this is not always the case, and *SHB Realisations Ltd v Cribbs Mall Nominees [2019] Lexis Citation 32* provides a recent high-profile example of a landlord forfeiting the lease of a major BHS store for breach of the keep-open covenant.

Other commercial opportunities

There may be other excellent commercial reasons to recover possession, of course. Typically:

- A right to forfeit in the context of a rising rental market holds out potential for a landlord to improve the quality of its investment by getting rid of an under-performing tenant, and re-letting to a new occupier with better covenant strength, at a higher rent.

- The landlord may have in mind a redevelopment of the property at some point in the future. Where a tenant within the property enjoys security of tenure under the *Landlord and Tenant Act 1954*, any breach of covenant presents an opportunity to forfeit the lease, recover possession, and re-let to a new tenant on a contracted-out basis. The landlord could then look forward in due course to recovering possession for the purposes of its redevelopment, without the uncertainties of opposing lease renewal.

- A feature of forfeiting by peaceable re-entry is that the landlord immediately becomes the owner of any items found on the premises which would otherwise have been tenant's fixtures (*Re Palmiero: Debtor 3666 of 1999 [1999] 3 EGLR 27*).

To expand very briefly on this point: when a tenant brings its own items into a leased property, they remain in the tenant's ownership provided they are not affixed (or 'annexed') to the property. Once annexed, they may become fixtures, depending on the method of annexation, and also the purpose of annexation; if so, they belong to the landlord, and must be left behind when the tenant vacates the premises at the end of the lease (subject to any contrary contractual provision). There is an exception to this rule in the sub-category of 'tenant's fixtures', which have been installed for the purposes of the tenant's trade, or for mere ornament, and which can be removed without causing undue damage to the premises or destroying the essential utility of the item itself. Such items can be removed by the tenant at any time up to the end of the lease, and once removed they revert to being the tenant's property. The extent of the items which are removeable on this basis can be surprisingly large, e.g. *Peel Land and Property (Ports No 3) Ltd v TS Sheerness Steel Ltd [2013] EWHC 1658 (Ch)*.

The *Re Palmiero* rule is potentially therefore very valuable, or at least useful: a landlord who forfeits the lease of a chip-shop, say, with an intention to re-let for the same use, should be able to re-let more readily, and potentially upon more advantageous terms, if the premises already include equipment such as a deep-fat fryer and a warming cabinet.

Drawing a line

Finally, there will always be situations in which the tenant's record of performance is so poor, with no prospect of improvement, or the breaches of covenant so serious, that whatever problems or drawbacks forfeiture may present, the landlord just needs to draw a line under the issue by getting rid of the tenant.

For all these reasons, the right to forfeit may be a very valuable property right.

Against

The matters counting against forfeiture are mostly just different aspects of one simple fact: the essence of forfeiture is recovery of vacant possession, and vacant property is usually a headache. Landlords do not invest in properties in order to hold them vacant, but to exploit their potential for rental growth by letting them out. A vacant, un-let property is a property which is not producing income; there will be a rental void before another tenant can be found, and letting expenses.

Market conditions

In a difficult letting market it may only be possible to let at a reduced rent, and perhaps to a tenant which the landlord would not accept in a better market. It may be difficult to find a tenant at all.

The popularity of forfeiture as a remedy therefore tends to come and go with market movements. In boom conditions landlords will enthusiastically forfeit leases when the opportunity arises; during a downturn they will look at other options. This can be seen in the absence from the law reports of any new cases on forfeiture for a period of years following the global financial crisis of 2007/8. It has only been in the past five years or so that new caselaw has begun to emerge.

Other factors may aggravate difficulties with re-letting:

- If the property has been left in a state of disrepair (which often accompanies termination by forfeiture), there may be no realistic prospect of recovering damages in a dilapidations claim against an impecunious former tenant. The landlord may not be able to re-let a dilapidated property on the basis that the new tenant takes on a full repairing obligation, but may instead have to concede an obligation limited by reference to a schedule of condition. Altern-atively, the landlord may have to spend its own money in putting the property into repair so as to succeed in re-letting.

• The impact of *ss. 42–51, Energy Act 2011*, and the *Energy Effi-ciency (Private Rented Property) (England and Wales) Regulations 2015, SI 2015/962* (commonly called the *MEES Regs 2015*) may mean that the landlord will not be permitted to re-let the premises until improvements have been made to their energy effi-ciency, again requiring it to spend money. The required improvements may be wholly unrelated to any disrepair for which the tenant is responsible, so that there is no prospect of the landlord recovering that expenditure.

• The property might be situated in an area which has declined in economic terms to such an extent that a commercial letting is no longer a realistic option. To obtain a return on its investment, the landlord would then have to incur expenditure in converting it to residential use.

Release of guarantors/former tenants

We have already mentioned the potential recourse against guarantors and former tenants, in considering the attractiveness of forfeiture for simple monetary default in the context of the other available remedies. The consequential release of such parties may be a powerful reason not to forfeit, since retaining their liability at least avoids the issue of rental void, and holds out the possibility of recovering damages for dilapida-tions, while allowing the landlord to defer any improvements to energy efficiency, or conversion to another use.

It should be mentioned that where forfeiture is effected by service of court proceedings rather than by peaceable re-entry, guarantors may remain liable until the proceedings are finally determined in the landlord's favour: *Ivory Gate Ltd v Spetale [1998] 2 EGLR 43*. Of course, the landlord cannot assume in such a case that there will ultimately be a successful application for relief from forfeiture, which might preserve the guarantors' liability in the long term.

Outgoings

While there is no money coming in from an un-let property, there will certainly be money going out. The landlord will be paying to insure the property, and will not be recovering the amount of the premiums from a tenant, as it would if the property were let. If the premises are part of a multi-let property to which the landlord provides services, the landlord will remain under obligations to provide those services to other tenants, but will have a shortfall in recovery of the cost as regards the un-let unit. It may be that the landlord's interest is itself leasehold, so that it continues to be liable for rent to a superior landlord. With no sub-tenant, that liability is not covered by a corresponding (or greater) income.

Perhaps the greatest concern currently for landlords, as regards the out-goings on un-let property, is business rates.

Business rates

The *Local Government Finance Act 1988* provides for business rates to be payable in respect of empty property, though until 2007 landlords were able to take advantage of various reliefs. The *Rating (Empty Properties) Act 2007* restricted those reliefs, with the aim of encouraging property owners not to leave their properties vacant. The *Non-domestic Rating (Unoccupied Property) (England) Regulations 2008* provide for what class of property is rateable and what properties are exempt.

Empty non-domestic properties are generally rateable if they have a building on them and are capable of beneficial occupation. The person liable to pay rates is the property owner, that is, the person entitled to possession of the property (*s.65(1), 1988 Act*). Where a lease has been terminated, it is the landlord who is liable to pay. The liability can be significant, particularly for larger properties: up to around 50% of the rental value.

The liability can perhaps be mitigated, since a number of rates avoidance schemes have emerged to take advantage of the available exemptions, and the developing caselaw suggests that the type which succeeds most reliably is that which utilises short-term lettings, often for storage purposes.

These schemes make use of the exemption which applies for the first three months that a property is vacant, or six months in the case of industrial or warehouse property. If during that exemption period there is a letting for at least six weeks, with rateable occupation, then a fresh exemption period begins once that letting comes to an end.

Under the typical short-term letting rates avoidance scheme, a 'storage company' is granted a six-month licence to occupy, containing mutual termination provisions. The company then goes into rateable occupation by dropping off a stack of pallets. After six weeks the arrangement is terminated, thereby re-setting the exemption. The landlord reimburses the storage company the rates liability for the six weeks, plus a profit element.

The caselaw concerning this sort of scheme is very helpful to the property owner. Even minimal use can be sufficient to amount to rateable occupation, and there is now effectively no substantial threshold. The courts have said that it must not be 'trifling' occupation, but this limitation has not so far been developed further, and with 0.2% occupation having been found to qualify (*Sunderland City Council v Stirling Investment Properties LLP [2013] EWHC 1413 (Admin)*), it is hard to see what would fail to amount to rateable occupation.

The courts have also said repeatedly that the fact that such schemes might be used for tax avoidance purposes is not a relevant consideration when determining whether there has been rateable occupation of the property. Rates mitigation schemes are not inherently wrong, and the acknowledged intention to avoid paying rates does not make them invalid.

However, some councils are looking to attack schemes of this nature by applying to the valuation office to have it assess a separate hereditament comprising only the occupied part of the premises. The council would then be entitled to business rates on the remaining empty space.

In any event, schemes of this sort are principally useful in relation to industrial and warehouse property. An office, leisure or retail property could not be used for storage without breaching planning restrictions, and possibly also contractual use restrictions, if the property were held on a lease. Apart from those issues, a retail unit used for storage would look very unappealing within a shopping centre.

Deemed utility supply contracts

Forfeiture of a lease will not, of course, terminate any utility supply contract which the former tenant has with a utility company such as an electricity supplier. However, at some point that supply contract is likely to be terminated, either by the tenant or by the supplier. That does not mean that there will be no supply to the property. Equipment such as burglar alarms and fire defence systems may well continue to use some power.

Paragraph 3 of *Schedule 6* to the *Electricity Act 1989* states that where there is a supply of electricity to premises without a contract being in place, a deemed contract can arise between the supplier and the occupier, or the owner if the premises are unoccupied. There is similar legislation for gas in *Paragraph 8* of *Schedule 2B* to the *Gas Act 1986*.

If the premises are unoccupied, then the amount of electricity or gas used should be minimal. However, if the meter is not read immediately after the termination of the old supply contract, the supplier may raise estimated demands based on previous usage, which may have been substantial.

Landlords can protect themselves by taking meter readings (and photographs) to avoid a supplier estimating and charging for the supply at the same level as when the premises were in use. This is especially important where the departing tenant had an enhanced-capacity supply due to the nature of their business.

Before making any payment, landlords should satisfy themselves that they are not being charged for any period before the former tenant's supply contract ended. They should ask for a copy of any document-ation of termination of the contract, and see whether that tallies with the date when the tenant departed the premises. They should also obtain a copy of the deemed contract, or details of its terms.

Security and insurers' requirements

A vacant property is naturally a security risk. Hand-in-hand with that fact goes insurers' requirements. If a property is vacant for a significant period, insurers will generally be entitled under the terms of the policy to be notified, and will require various steps to be followed. If all of this is not done, cover may be jeopardised.

Requirements may be fairly minimal for a low-value, low-risk property: draining the water system, sealing letterboxes and regular inspections. For substantial high-risk properties, they may include installing or upgrading physical measures such as locks, window-bars, CCTV and alarm systems, placing concrete blocks at the site perimeter to prevent vehicle access, and engaging a 24-hour security presence. The expense may be considerable.

Tenant's goods

The landlord becomes an involuntary bailee of any tenant's goods found on the premises following forfeiture, and this is often a headache. Because being a bailee involves a limited duty of care, it is prudent to insure the goods, though the landlord cannot claim the cost from the tenant. The goods can be removed from the property and put into storage if necessary, though the tenant must be told where they have gone, and any storage costs will not be recoverable from the tenant. It is obvious sense to prepare an inventory of the goods, to prevent dispute. The landlord must give the tenant access to collect its goods at any reasonable time. and cannot dispose of the goods without serving on the tenant a notice under the *Torts (Interference With Goods) Act 1977*. If the goods include computers, hard drives, disks, etc., there may be data protection issues in relation to disposal of the goods. (These issues will be addressed more fully when considering forfeiture by peaceable re-entry in Chapter 7).

Conclusion

Many of the 'against' considerations are management headaches, rather than really significant problems, and can by managed and mitigated by exercise of the proper due diligence. Others are more important. Which will carry more weight in any particular situation, and whether they may be outweighed by one or more 'for' factors, is completely fact-dependent.

Landlords will generally embark upon forfeiture for one of two reasons: either they genuinely want to recover possession, or they believe that the tenant will not want to lose the lease, and will therefore put right any breaches of covenant and obtain relief from forfeiture. For their advisers, it is important to ensure that the landlord is aware that recovery of possession is far from guaranteed, because of the availability of relief from forfeiture (there is perhaps consolation in the reflection that the successful applicant for relief will invariably be required to pay all the landlord's costs on an indemnity basis). The landlord should also be advised, perhaps even more importantly, that the tenant may accept the forfeiture, walk away from the property, and leave the landlord to pick up all of the vacant property issues, without having remedied the breaches of covenant.

The observation made in Chapter 1 will bear repeating: forfeiture should be undertaken in the understanding that the tenant will probably obtain relief if it remedies the breaches of covenant, but also in the acceptance that it may not apply for relief, and that the outcome may be a vacant property.

Summary

In deciding whether to forfeit a lease, factors which are likely to be important, and which should be discussed with landlord clients, are:

<u>For</u>

- It can be a very quick, cheap and effective remedy in case of simple monetary default, though the advantages of other remedies should also be considered

- As regards other types of breach of covenant, such as alienation breaches, or breach of keep-open covenant, it is often the most effective remedy

- Forfeiture may enable the landlord to take advantage of very valuable commercial opportunities to re-let on better terms, or to obtain possession for redevelopment purposes

- It draws a line under problems with unsatisfactory tenants or serious breaches of covenant

<u>Against</u>

- Re-letting may be difficult or impossible, without unrecoverable expenditure on the landlord's part, and in the meantime the property is not producing income

- Forfeiture will release third parties such as guarantors and former tenants who may remain liable to perform the tenant's covenants under the lease

- The landlord will continue to be liable for outgoings on the property, such as insurance premiums, service costs, head-rent, and (most importantly) business rates. Rates avoidance schemes exist, but may be difficult or impossible to take advantage of, depending upon the property

- Liability may arise to utility suppliers under deemed supply contracts

- Insurers' requirements in relation to the property can involve significant expenditure

- Disposing of tenant's goods left at the property can often be problematic

CHAPTER FOUR
WAIVER OF THE RIGHT
TO FORFEIT

This chapter covers the risk of the landlord inadvertently losing the right to forfeit by means of waiver, including the circumstances in which the risk may arise, what amounts to waiver, and what may be done to avoid it. It also considers the effect of waiver, and the distinction made between so-called 'continuing' and 'once-and-for-all' breaches of covenant.

It follows from the principle that a right to forfeit renders the lease, not void, but voidable at the landlord's option, that the landlord must elect whether to exercise the right or not. Since the courts "*lean against forfeiture*", an election not to forfeit has come to be considered by the courts as irrevocable. The choice for the landlord is thus between two irrevocable courses, since once forfeiture is effected, it too is irrevocable. This makes for a high stakes game, but the real practical problem for the landlord is that the courts may construe an election not to forfeit out of conduct or words which were not informed by any inkling of forfeiture.

The general principle is that once a landlord has acquired knowledge of the facts giving rise to a right to forfeit, it is put to its election whether or not to allow the lease to continue. Any act or statement after then which expressly or implicitly acknowledges the continuing existence of the lease will be taken as a choice to allow it to continue, and will waive the right to forfeit.

The right to forfeit can thus be lost easily and inadvertently, by the operation of the doctrine of waiver. This is one of the most problematic aspects of the present law of forfeiture. The right to forfeit is potentially a valuable one, as we have said before, and until such time as the landlord has taken a firm decision not to forfeit, it is important not to lose it. The risk of waiver is therefore something which the landlord must guard against as soon as the existence of the right to forfeit becomes known.

The risk period

The risk period in which the right to forfeit might be lost begins upon the acquisition of the relevant knowledge. The risk period ends either (a) upon forfeiture, since the right, having been exercised, can no longer be waived (*Civil Service Co-operative Society v McGrigor's Trustee [1923] 2 Ch 347*), or (b) upon the landlord taking a firm and settled decision not to forfeit, in which case waiver of the right is not a concern.

It is knowledge of the facts which constitute the right to forfeit which is required, not a legal conclusion that there is a breach of covenant, or that there is a right to forfeit (*David Blackstone Ltd v Burnetts (West End) Ltd [1973] 1 WLR 1487*). It is sufficient if the landlord is aware of facts that pointed to a breach of covenant or which should put him on inquiry as to the nature of the breach (*Metropolitan Properties Co Ltd v Cordery [1979] 2 EGLR 78*). The degree of knowledge required is accordingly slight, and a practical consequence of this is that there may often be a period between the acquisition of the relevant knowledge and the landlord realising that it has a right to forfeit, during which time the risk of waiver is present, but the landlord will not have been in a position to take any steps to guard against it.

The risk is all the greater because the knowledge need not be acquired by the landlord personally; it might be that of a managing agent retained by the landlord. It could equally be that of a solicitor, or even a caretaker, so long as it is a person with some degree of involvement in the management of the property on the landlord's behalf (*Central Estates (Belgravia) Ltd v Woolgar (No. 2) [1972] 3 All ER 610*).

Waiver is a risk even though, because a s.146 notice has not been served, or the required 'reasonable time' has not yet elapsed after service of a s.146 notice, the landlord is not yet in a position to forfeit the lease. This issue arose in *Stemp v 6 Ladbroke Gardens Ltd [2018] UKUT 375 (LC)*.

In that case, the landlord demanded a substantial amount of service charge, which the tenant did not pay. A right to forfeit arose. However, under *s.81(1), Housing Act 1996* a landlord may not forfeit a lease for non-payment of service charge until the First-tier Tribunal has determined that the service charge was due. The landlord applied to the Tribunal for a determination, and while that application was pending, it served a second demand for service charge. The consequence of that was to waive the existing right to forfeit.

The tenant subsequently paid all service charge, but the landlord sought to recover its legal costs incurred in contemplation of forfeiture, pursuant to a clause in the lease. The Upper Tribunal determined that the costs were due, but only up to the date of the second demand, since the waiver meant that forfeiture was an impossibility after that date.

The landlord argued that its ability to forfeit was subject to a statutory moratorium pursuant to *s.81(1)* of the 1996 Act, and also under *s.146, Law of Property Act 1925*, because it could not forfeit until it had served a s.146 notice and allowed a reasonable time to elapse. A period of time, perhaps a very lengthy one, will elapse between the date on which the contractual entitlement to forfeit a lease in respect of a breach of covenant arises and the date when the statutory restriction on the exercise of that right is lifted. The landlord's argument was that until the statutory moratorium had ended, thus enabling it to forfeit, the right to forfeit could not be waived.

The Upper Tribunal disagreed, holding that "*…it is possible to make an unequivocal choice between two inconsistent rights prior to being in a position immediately to exercise each of them*".

What amounts to waiver

To constitute waiver, the relevant act or statement must have been communicated to the tenant: *London & County (A&D) Ltd v Wilfred Sportsman Ltd [1971] 1 Ch 764.*

Time-related tests

The act of waiver must acknowledge the existence of the lease at a time after there was a right to forfeit. There are, in effect, two time-related tests to be met before there can be a waiver. For an action or statement to amount to waiver, it must:

(a) have occurred *after the time of acquisition of the relevant know-ledge*, and

(b) imply continuation of the lease at a time *after the right to forfeit arose*.

Demand/acceptance of rent

The classic instance of waiver is sending out a demand for rent falling due after the right to forfeit arose, or accepting payment of it (*Greenwood Reversions Ltd v World Entertainment Foundation* Ltd *[2008] H.L.R. 31*; *R Square Properties Ltd v Reach Learning Ltd [2017] EWHC 2947 (Ch)*). It is settled law that either would amount to a waiver of the right to forfeit. The same would apply to suing for that rent: *Dendy v Nicholl (1856) 4 CB (NS) 376*.

The landlord cannot protect itself by accepting payment of rent on a 'without prejudice' basis (*Segal Securities v Thoseby [1963] 1 All ER 500*). Some leases provide that demand or acceptance of rent shall be deemed not to be a waiver. By analogy with *R v Paulson [1921] 1 AC 271*, it is thought that such provisions are ineffective; a landlord cannot provide contractually that black is white.

Rent due prior to right to forfeit

The landlord can accept or pursue rent falling due prior to the date when the right to forfeit arose, without any waiver. For example, if £5000 rent falls due on 25 March, but under the terms of the lease the right to forfeit does not arise for another 14 days, the landlord can chase that payment or even sue for the rent at any time without thereby waiving the right to forfeit (*Re A Debtor [1996] 1 All ER 691; Stephens v Junior Army and Navy Stores Ltd [1914] 2 Ch 516*). This is because an express or implicit assertion that a rent instalment fell due on 25 March carries no implication as to the continuation of the lease at any time after 8 April, when the right to forfeit arose. The rent instalment might relate to the period up to and including 23 June, but the entire sum fell due as a debt on 25 March.

Appropriation

To continue that example, assume now that (i) the landlord sends out a rent review trigger notice in May, in relation to a forthcoming rent review, thus waiving the right to forfeit in relation to the non-payment of the March quarter's rent; and (ii) the tenant does not pay the June or September rent instalments on the due dates either, but tenders a cheque for a quarter's rent, £5000, at the end of October.

If the landlord accepts the cheque in payment of the September quarter's rent, then as regards the right to forfeit for non-payment of the June quarter's rent, both time-related tests have been met, and it will have been waived (the right to forfeit for the March quarter's rent having already been waived by the rent review trigger notice). Since the September quarter's rent will now have been paid, there will be no right to forfeit at all, until some future rent instalment remains unpaid more than 14 days after the due date.

The question which must be considered in such a case is whether the tenant has 'appropriated' the rent to the September quarter (for the principles of appropriation see *Thomas v Ken Thomas Ltd [2006] EWCA Civ 1504*). There are at this stage three quarters' rent due and unpaid, for March, June and September, and if the tenant has not identified in any way which one the payment relates to, then the landlord can 'appropriate' it, and accept it as payment of the March quarter, in relation to which the right to forfeit has already been waived. That will leave intact the two rights to forfeit in relation to the June and September rent instalments.

If the tenant sends a cheque with a letter saying "here's the September rent", it is not open to the landlord to accept it as payment for the March quarter. It can only be accepted as payment for the September quarter, thus waiving the right to forfeit in relation to the June rent. The landlord can only preserve the ability to forfeit for the June rent, in that situation, by returning the cheque.

In reality, of course, payment may very likely be made by bank transfer, with no convenient covering letter. The payment reference, though, may be taken from the September invoice, which might easily be a sufficient 'appropriation'. Other facts might point that way, too. If a tenant owes two quarters' rent at £5000 each, plus service charge amounting to £3722.31, and makes a payment for £3722.31 without any other indication of what the payment relates to, there is an obvious inference.

Electronic payment of rent

Tenants may very often be required in modern leases to pay by bank transfer or standing order, so that money is received directly into the landlord's bank account, with no opportunity to refuse it. If the landlord cannot 'appropriate' the payment so as to preserve a right to forfeit, attempts should be made to return the payment promptly, which should avoid waiver (*John Lewis Properties v Viscount Chelsea [1993] 34 EG 116*).

If it proves impossible to return the payment, it is evidentially useful, though by no means essential, if the landlord or its agent is able to place the payment into a separate 'suspense account', pending determination of the dispute. That indicates that the payment is not being treated as part of the general receipts for the landlord.

Combining forfeiture and arrears claims

After a landlord has effected forfeiture, by peaceable re-entry or by serving proceedings claiming possession, it can bring a claim for any outstanding rent which accrued due prior to the re-entry: *Hartshorne v*

Watson (1838) 4 Bing NC 178. Waiver, of course, is then no longer an issue.

Neither is waiver a problem where the landlord brings forfeiture proceedings based upon arrears of rent, and includes a claim for those arrears. Indeed, this is absolutely normal procedure. As stated above, because the rent accrued due prior to the landlord acquiring the right to forfeit, there is no waiver.

Where there is a problem, though, is in the case of forfeiture proceedings which include a claim for arrears falling due after the right to forfeit arose in relation to a different breach, upon which the proceedings rest. Say, for instance, that a sub-lease was granted in breach of covenant on 10 May. The landlord found out about it shortly afterwards, and put a stop on the rent account, so that no further demands went out, and no rent was accepted. The landlord served a s.146 notice on 1 June, and waited two months before issuing forfeiture proceedings on 1 August. In those proceedings, it included a claim for the rent due on 24 June. Did the inclusion of the rent claim waive the right to forfeit?

In *Penton v Barnett [1898] 1 QB 276* the answer was 'no', however the breach in that case was of the repairing covenant. As discussed below, that is regarded as a 'continuing' breach, and in such cases the landlord's right to possession is unaffected by any act of waiver. In the case of a 'once-and-for-all' breach (such as the grant of the sub-lease in our example), the court said: "*the state of things might have been different*".

It is safest, therefore, to avoid including arrears claims in such cases.

Use of Commercial Rent Arrears Recovery

Under the old law of distress for rent, a landlord who instructed bailiffs to levy distress would waive any right to forfeit the lease, irrespective of when the arrears fell due. It might be the case, as in our example above, that the arrears of rent had fallen due on 25 March, before the right to forfeit arose on 8 April, so that demanding payment, or suing for the arrears, would not acknowledge the continuing existence of the lease beyond the latter date; nevertheless, the act of levying distress for that sum on 10 May would be an acknowledgement that the lease was continuing on 10 May, since distress could only be levied if there was a subsisting landlord and tenant relationship.

Brar v Thirunavukkrasu [2019] EWCA Civ 2032 has confirmed that the same applies to the exercise of Commercial Rent Arrears Recovery ("CRAR"), the statutory remedy which replaced distress for rent, under the *Tribunals, Courts and Enforcement Act 2007*. CRAR, unlike distress for rent, can be used after termination of a lease in certain circumstances, but is specifically excluded after forfeiture. It follows that exercise of CRAR constitutes an unequivocal representation that the lease is continuing at the time of instructing the enforcement agent, and waives any right to forfeit.

Other acts of waiver

As regards alleged waiver otherwise than by demand or acceptance of rent, it was observed in the *Greenwood Reversions* case that it is necessary:

> "*to consider objectively whether in all the circumstances the act relied on as constituting waiver is so unequivocal that when considered objectively it could only be regarded as being consistent with the lease continuing*".

Whether or not there has been a waiver turns entirely on the quality of the act in question, in respect of which the motive or intention of the landlord is irrelevant (*Central Estates (Belgravia) Ltd v Woolgar (No 2) [1972] 3 All ER 610*).

Examples

Common examples of conduct which will amount to waiver are:

- Exercising a right to carry out repairs in default of the tenant doing so: *Doe d. Rutzen v Lewis (1836) 111 ER 1170.*

- Seeking to enforce tenant's covenants in the lease by means of injunction: *Calabar Properties Ltd v Seagull Autos Ltd [1969] 1 Ch 451.*

- Serving notice to quit: *Marche v Christodoulakis (1984) 64 TLR 466.*

- Granting a licence to assign or sub-let.

- Exercising a right to inspect the premises.

- Serving notice under *s.25, Landlord and Tenant Act 1954.*

- Initiating or progressing a forthcoming rent review

That list is illustrative, rather than comprehensive, and the landlord needs to have regard to the general principle: anything that the landlord does or says which necessarily implies the continued existence of the lease will suffice. The best approach for the landlord and those acting on its behalf is: if it is something that you would not do or say if the lease were at an end, then do not do it or say it.

Waiver by agent

Like the acquisition of knowledge, the waiver need not be effected by the landlord itself, but may be done by someone acting on the landlord's behalf, even without the landlord's knowledge. The landlord's right to forfeit could be waived by the knowledge of one person and the act of another, without either of them, or the landlord personally, ever being aware of having had the right. As Lord Denning MR said in *Central Estates (Belgravia) Ltd v Woolgar*:

> "*The principal cannot escape the doctrine of waiver by saying that one clerk had the knowledge and the other received the rent. They must be regarded as one for this purpose. The landlords' agents knew the position and they accepted the rent with knowledge. That is a waiver.*"

An illustrative example may help to underline the absurdity of this:

(a) *A managing agent makes a routine inspection visit to retail premises. In the course of his visit he notices that the tenant has installed some air-conditioning plant on a flat roof to the rear of the premises. He knows that there has been no attempt to obtain the landlord's consent to this.*

   Installing the air-conditioning was a breach of the alterations covenant in the lease, which prohibits all but internal, non-structural alterations to the premises, except with the landlord's prior written consent.

   The knowledge of the agent is attributed to the landlord, and there is now a risk of waiver. The agent need not have concluded that there has been a breach of the alterations covenant, nor that a right to forfeit has arisen. Those are legal conclusions. The agent has knowledge of the facts which constitute the breach of covenant, and which therefore give rise to the right to forfeit, and so the landlord is at risk.

(b) *The agent's visit took place on a Tuesday. On the Friday of the same week, the accounts department of the same firm of agents, not having been instructed otherwise, sends out a demand for the rent which will fall due 28 days later. That is clearly an acknowledgement of the continuing existence of the lease, and is unmistakably an act of waiver. The act of the agent is attributed to the landlord, and the right to forfeit has now been waived. It does not matter that the accounts department knew nothing of the breach of alterations covenant, nor that there was no intention in their mind or the landlord's to waive the right to forfeit.*

(c) *The landlord finds out about the unlawful alterations a week afterwards, when he receives a report from the agent, but as far as the law is concerned, he is taken to have already weighed up the options and decided not to forfeit the lease.*

Landlord performing lease covenants

The decision in *Stemp v 6 Ladbroke Gardens Ltd [2018] UKUT 375 (LC)* features one aspect which is rather more encouraging for landlords. The Upper Tribunal held that where a landlord who is proceeding to forfeit a lease relies on the lease terms to perform its own obligations (in this instance, maintenance of the property), this is not an act which unequivocally assumes the continued existence of the lease, and will not necessarily amount to a waiver of the right to forfeit. This means that a landlord is not put in the practically undesirable position of having to choose between performance of its own leasehold covenants (risking waiver of the right to forfeit) or refusal to do so (avoiding such a risk, but exposing itself to a claim for breach of the lease).

The decision was fact-dependent, though, and should not be regarded as establishing a general rule. It should be considered in the context of other caselaw relating to the so-called 'twilight period', discussed in Chapter 6.

Avoidance of waiver

We have seen that the landlord cannot prevent waiver by accepting payment of rent on a 'without prejudice' basis (*Segal Securities v Thoseby [1963] 1 All ER 500*). In the same way, if a landlord who has a right to forfeit sends out a rent review trigger notice, it is probable that it cannot avoid thereby waiving its right by serving the notice under the heading 'without prejudice to the right to forfeit', or some such formula.

Since waiver may be effected not only by acts, but also by statements, the landlord and its advisers must be very careful about how they express themselves in dealings with the tenant. The tenant in *Stemp v 6 Ladbroke Gardens Ltd* had argued that various letters from the landlord had waived the right to forfeit, since some had been addressed "*Dear Leaseholders*", some referred to leasehold covenants or potential liability for service charges, or to "*your Lease*", and another was stated to be from "*your Landlord*". The judge gave the argument fairly short shrift. The tenant was in fact the leaseholder during the period, and it was simple good sense to refer to them as such. However, it is not uncommon for tenants to cite this sort of language as amounting to waiver, and the only way the landlord can avoid having to deal with the argument is to have no contact with the tenant.

While negotiations with the tenant may well include statements which amount to waiver, for the tenant to establish that there has indeed been a waiver it is necessary to identify the actual statements, and not simply to rely on the fact of negotiations having taken place. Since the court cannot have regard to 'without prejudice' correspondence, it ought to be possible for negotiations to proceed on that basis without risking waiver (*Re National Jazz Centre Ltd [1988] 2 EGLR 57*).

Most landlords and their advisers will nevertheless be very cautious about this. The privilege in relation to 'without prejudice' communications extends to settlement negotiations. In the course of correspondence concerning the breach which has given rise to the right to forfeit, it is quite possible that settlement negotiations will be mixed with other content, particularly where the correspondence is being conducted otherwise than through lawyers. That gives scope for argument that the privilege does not extend to particular statements or items of correspondence, and means there is potential for waiver arising out of such statements or items.

The net effect is that once a landlord knows of a right to forfeit, unless and until it is decided that there will be no forfeiture the safe course is to put a stop on the tenant's rent account, so that no more demands will be sent and no more rent will be accepted (advice which is never welcome to a landlord). Also, the landlord and its agents are best advised to avoid any contact with the tenant or its advisers, and instead refer them to the landlord's solicitors.

This is highly impractical and inconvenient. For one thing, while it is easy to advise a client that neither they nor anyone acting on their behalf should have any contact with the tenant, it may not be so easy for the landlord to ensure that that advice is implemented. There is potentially a large number of people who might ordinarily have contact with the tenant, from different departments and personnel within a firm of managing agents, to caretakers and shopping centre managers, and all must clearly understand that they should firmly refuse to speak to or correspond with the tenant. The tenant is likely to be quite insistent.

For another thing, it means that matters which could perhaps be resolved quickly in 'without prejudice' correspondence or discussions cannot be dealt with in that way, if the landlord is to be confident that the right to forfeit is preserved. The landlord should instead forfeit the lease, and then negotiate the terms for relief. The risk, of course, is that the tenant will accept the forfeiture, leaving the landlord with a vacant property. From the tenant's point of view, it can be frustrating and inexplicable that the landlord chooses to forfeit the lease rather than resolve the matter by negotiation. However, that is the necessary con-sequence of the doctrine of waiver.

Alienation breaches

A particularly difficult issue can arise as regards alienation breaches, when the landlord is subject to the duties in *s.1(3), Landlord and Tenant Act 1988*, but needs to avoid waiving a right to forfeit the lease. Under *s.1(3)*, where (as is almost always the case) landlord's consent to an assignment or sub-letting is not to be unreasonably withheld, the landlord is under a number of duties:

- to give consent unless it is reasonable not to do so;

- if imposing conditions upon a grant of consent, only to impose reasonable ones;

- when refusing consent, to give its reasons for doing so;

- when imposing conditions, to stipulate what the conditions are; and

- to give its decision in writing within a reasonable time.

Breach of any of the statutory duties entitles the tenant to claim damages under *s.4*.

Difficulty arises where the right to forfeit is directly related to an application for consent to assign or sub-let. Retrospective applications for consent are irregular, in the sense that the lease will usually require landlord's "*prior*" consent, but they are not uncommon. It is frequently the case that, in a business acquisition, time does not allow for the seller to go through the process of applying for landlord's consent to assign each of the leases it holds, and dealing with the objections of each landlord. Instead, the deal proceeds, including assignment of the leases (or perhaps the grant by the seller to the buyer of licences to occupy, pending assignment) and consent is then applied for retrospectively. The landlord is thus presented with a breach of covenant as well as an application for consent.

Another situation which sometimes crops up is that a tenant applies for consent to assign, and the landlord objects because it is not satisfied with the financial status of the assignee. Negotiations as to providing acceptable security ensue. Tenant and assignee both take the view that the landlord is plainly unreasonable, and that accordingly there will be no breach of covenant in simply going ahead with the assignment, which they proceed to do. From the landlord's point of view, since it believes that it is not being unreasonable, this is a breach of covenant, and gives rise to a right to forfeit.

The landlord faces an uncomfortable dilemma in such situations. On the one hand, a concern about the covenant strength of the assignee is important, and the most reliable remedy, if an acceptable compromise cannot be reached, is forfeiture. On the other, given the many potential disadvantages to forfeiture, the landlord may ultimately be prepared to allow the assignment to proceed, if appropriate security can be negotiated. The landlord may want, therefore, to preserve the ability to forfeit the lease, while attempting to negotiate acceptable security.

'Without prejudice' negotiations, though, run the risk of waiver. Ideally, the landlord would have no contact with the tenant whatsoever. However, the duties under s.1(3) continue to apply: the landlord must engage in the process sufficiently to establish whether its objections are reasonable, and must deliver its decision within a reasonable time. If it fails to do so, it risks a claim for damages.

There is no completely reliable way of squaring this circle. Perhaps the best the landlord can do is (a) make sure that all correspondence is 'without prejudice', and hope that this gives some protection, and (b) explicitly limit its continuing consideration of the application to the possibility of an application for relief from forfeiture. Its position might be set out like this: the landlord intends to forfeit the lease; as and when it does so, the landlord recognises that the tenant might make an application for relief from forfeiture, which might succeed; therefore the lease is potentially good, and purely on the basis that there might be a successful application for relief, the landlord continues to engage with the application for consent.

Effect of waiver

The effect of waiver is not to deprive the landlord of all remedies in relation to the breach of covenant, but only of the right to forfeit. Depending on the nature of the breach, the landlord might still be able to use Commercial Rent Arrears Recovery, serve a statutory demand, sue for debt or damages, or seek an injunction.

It would be possible for a landlord to 'waive the breach' (an expression in common but inaccurate use when speaking of waiver of the right to forfeit), meaning that it waives *all* remedies in relation to it. It would even be possible to 'waive the covenant', effectively writing the covenant out of the lease for the future. However, either course would generally require unequivocal express notification, and could not be done easily or inadvertently, as is the case with waiver of the right to forfeit.

Continuing breaches

The law makes a distinction between 'continuing' and 'once-and-for-all' breaches of covenant, in relation to the operation of waiver. In the case of a continuing breach, a fresh right to forfeit arises immediately after each act of waiver, so that the right to forfeit cannot be lost.

A once-and-for-all breach may be a breach of:

(i) an obligation to do something by a particular time. That might be an obligation to do something by a specified date, such as paying the rent on the quarter-day (the common practice of speaking of the tenant 'being in arrears', as a continuing state of affairs, can be misleading in this respect). It might also include an obligation to do something which ought to be done within a reasonable time, for example to use insurance monies in rebuilding and repairing the demised premises (*Farimani v Gates [1984] 2 EGLR 66*). Once the date or the reasonable time has passed without performance of the obligation, then it has been breached, and cannot be breached again.

(ii) an obligation which is not time-limited: that is, it applies throughout the term of the lease. However, in that case the breach itself must be complete and not ongoing. A prohibition on assigning the lease without landlord's consent, for example, applies throughout the term, but as soon as the tenant assigns the lease without consent there is a complete, perfected breach.

A continuing breach, on the other hand, is a breach of:

(iii) an obligation which applies throughout the term and is not time-limited, but where the breach itself is ongoing. Breach of a covenant only to use premises for a particular purpose (*Cooper v Henderson (1982) 263 EG 592*), and breach of a covenant to keep in repair (*Penton v Barnett [1898] 1 QB 276*), are considered to be continuing breaches.

A useful rule of thumb for telling the difference between (ii) and (iii) is to consider whether the obligation is positive or negative in nature: a positive obligation to keep premises in repair throughout the term of the lease will be continually breached in each instant that the property is in disrepair. A breach of a negative covenant not to assign without landlord's consent, however, while it applies throughout the term, is breached once-and-for-all as soon as the prohibition has been broken. This is not a perfect guide, though, since use covenants are most commonly couched in a negative form ("*not to use the premises other than for the business of a greengrocer*"), but a breach will generally be considered to be a continuing one, nevertheless.

Deciding which category a particular breach falls into must always be a matter of construction: while alienation breaches are generally considered to be once-and-for-all, breach of a covenant against *sharing* occupation might well be considered to be continuing. There might be a difference in this respect between a covenant "*not to use the premises other than for the business of a greengrocer*" and a covenant "*not to change the use of the premises from that of a greengrocer*".

As noted above, in the case of a continuing breach a fresh right to forfeit arises immediately after each act of waiver, and the right to forfeit cannot be lost. While a landlord can therefore generally be relaxed about the issue of waiver in relation to continuing breaches, it should not drop its guard entirely.

- For one thing, there might still be an issue about compliance with *s.146, Law of Property Act 1925*. Where a continuing breach of covenant exists, and the landlord, having served a s.146 notice, then commits an act of waiver, is there a need to serve a new s.146 notice in relation to the new right to forfeit which arose immediately after the waiver? The conventional view is that there is no such requirement, but doubt has been cast on this in *Farimani v Gates [1984] 2 EGLR 66*. In practical terms this could be important. The breach complained of might be serious disrepair, and the reasonable time which should elapse before forfeiture might in such a case be very lengthy, perhaps as much as a year. If, in month 11 of that year, the tenant meanwhile having done nothing to address the disrepair, the landlord were to commit an act of waiver, the inconvenience in having to serve a second s.146 notice and wait another year before forfeiture would be considerable.

• Also, if there is a once-and-for-all breach, but also a continuing breach which is consequential upon and integral to the once-and-for-all breach, waiver may have the effect of preventing forfeiture in reliance upon the continuing breach as well. In *Griffin v Tomkins (1880) 42 LT 359*, the tenants converted the premises into a shop, which was a once-and-for-all breach of the alterations covenant. The purpose of the conversion was to carry on business as plumbers, which they subsequently did. That was a continuing breach of the user covenant. It was held that acceptance of rent by the landlord, in knowledge of the breaches, prevented forfeiture in reliance upon both breaches, the once-and-for-all alterations breach and the continuing user breach.

Where a continuing breach of covenant exists forfeiture may, exceptionally, be prevented by repeated acts of waiver over a very long period, leading to an inference of waiver of the covenant itself. An example of this is *Gibbon v Payne (1905) 22 TLR 54*, where the landlord acquiesced in the tenant's breach of covenant for almost 40 years. On the other hand, a 17-year period of acquiescence did not prevent forfeiture in *Lloyds Bank v Jones [1955] 2 QB 298*.

Summary

Once knowledge of facts amounting to a breach of covenant has been acquired by the landlord or its agent, there is a risk that the right to forfeit may be lost by waiver. Any act or statement by or on behalf of the landlord which acknowledges the continuing existence of the lease after the date on which the right to forfeit arose will constitute waiver.

Waiver only ceases to be a risk after forfeiture has been effected, or once the landlord takes a firm decision not to forfeit.

Waiver is conventionally avoided by ceasing to demand or accept rent from the tenant, and by avoiding any contact with them. This is both difficult, and practically very inconvenient.

It is only in the case of 'continuing' breaches of covenant (principally breach of repair covenant or user covenant) that waiver is not a concern, since a new right to forfeit arises immediately after each act of waiver.

CHAPTER FIVE
MATTERS PRELIMINARY TO
FORFEITURE

This chapter deals with matters which should be addressed preparatory to forfeiture, including some specific matters affecting the ability to forfeit for arrears of rent, and for breach of repairing covenant, but principally the requirement, in most cases of forfeiture, for service of a notice under s.146, Law of Property Act 1925.

This book deals with forfeiture of commercial leases, but it should be borne in mind that additional protections apply to residential tenants, largely in the form of qualifying conditions which must be satisfied, and preliminary formalities which must be completed, before forfeiture is permitted. These are summarised briefly in Chapter 1, and are not dealt with further here.

Section 146 notices

Nature of notice requirement

Apart from a few exceptions, where a landlord intends to forfeit a lease, it cannot do so unless it has first served on the tenant a notice under *s.146, Law of Property Act 1925*. This is a warning notice which specifies the breach of covenant complained of, requires the tenant to remedy it, if it is remediable, and requires the tenant to pay compensation for it. The notice will inform the tenant that the landlord intends to forfeit the lease if the breach is not remedied within a reasonable time.

If the landlord is complaining of breach of repairing covenant, and if the *Leasehold Property (Repairs) Act 1938* applies, the notice must additionally contain prominent wording notifying the tenant of its rights under the Act. The procedure under the 1938 Act will be outlined more fully later in this chapter.

Other than that requirement, there is no prescribed form for s.146 notices, though the drafting is fairly standard. An illustrative example of a s.146 notice is given in the Appendix.

Under *s.146(3)*, landlords are entitled to recover the costs of the preparation and service of a s.146 notice if they waive the relevant breach at the tenant's request, or if the court grants the tenant relief from forfeiture. Given the limited nature of this entitlement, most leases provide that the landlord may recover the costs of serving a s.146 notice, whatever the circumstances or subsequent events.

Exceptions to requirement for notice

The chief exception to the requirement for a s.146 notice is in the case of forfeiture in reliance upon non-payment of rent (*s.146(11)*). Forfeiture is commonly regarded as the ultimate security for payment of rent, hence no barrier is placed in the landlord's way, when exercising the right to forfeit for this purpose. No warning notice is given to the tenant, and forfeiture may be effected by peaceable re-entry, so that the tenant who does not pay the rent on time risks arriving at their business premises to find that the locks have been changed and their lease has been terminated. The flipside to this coin is the automatic grant of relief upon payment of the arrears.

There are further very limited exceptions to the requirement for a s.146 notice, in relation to certain bankruptcy situations, and breach of certain types of covenant in mining leases, contained in *s.146(8), (9)* and *(10)*. The exceptions in relation to bankruptcy are considered in Chapter 11.

Premature notice

In *Toms v Ruberry [2019] EWCA Civ 128*, the landlord of licensed premises attempted to forfeit the lease in reliance upon various breaches of covenant, broadly relating to disrepair. The lease permitted service by the landlord of a contractual 'tenant default notice', specifying a time within which breaches referred to in the notice should be remedied.

Should the tenant fail to do so, then the landlord would be entitled to re-enter upon the premises and forfeit the lease.

The landlord served a tenant default notice, and simultaneously a s.146 notice. The tenant was required to remedy the breaches of covenant within seven weeks. She failed to do so, and after the expiry of that time the landlord commenced forfeiture proceedings.

The landlord's claim was dismissed, despite the tenant's failure to remedy the breaches of covenant, on the basis that service of the s.146 notice had been premature. Until the time for compliance with the contractual tenant default notice had elapsed, there was no right to forfeit. The court rejected an argument that a s.146 notice could validly be given before there was any right to forfeit.

It is unusual for leases to contain these additional procedural steps, so the point may not arise very often.

<u>On whom served</u>

If the lease is held by joint tenants, the notice must be served upon all of them (*Blewett v Blewett [1936] 2 All ER 188*).

Although forfeiture of the lease will also generally bring to an end inferior interests such as sub-leases, mortgages or charges granted out of the lease, there is no statutory requirement that notice be served upon any sub-tenant, mortgagee or chargee. Lenders will usually include in their standard terms a requirement that notices are passed to them immediately, but of course that does not ensure that they will be. It would be preferable from their point of view to obtain an obligation on the landlord to give them copies of any notice served, but the landlord has no reason to be involved in documentation of the mortgage or charge, and no reason other than goodwill to agree such a term.

Often landlords may take the initiative in involving mortgagees, and notify them of any arrears or other breach of covenant. The mortgagee will wish to preserve its security, and is likely to pressure the tenant/borrower to tackle the issue. The mortgagee may pay any arrears, and add the amount, together with any costs, to the mortgage debt. Even if not involved in this way, sub-tenants and mortgagees may be able to protect their interests later on in the process, by applying for relief. However, the Council of Mortgage Lenders has reported that its members often find out about forfeiture of a mortgaged lease only when contacted by the Land Registry during the process of closing title, which may be long after the forfeiture.

If the breach of covenant complained of is an assignment of the lease without the landlord's consent, the s.146 notice must be served on the assignee, because even though the assignment was unlawful, it will have transferred the legal estate to the assignee: *Fuller v Judy Properties Ltd [1992] 14 EG 106*. There is an important caveat, though, in the case of a registered lease: there, the legal estate does not pass until registration has been completed (*Brown & Root Technology Ltd v Sun Alliance Assurance Co Ltd (1997) The Times, 27 January*), also *Sackville UK Property Select II (GP) No.1 Ltd v Robertson Taylor Insurance Brokers Ltd [2018] EWHC 122 (Ch)*. Therefore, until the assignee has been registered as proprietor the s.146 notice should be served on the assignor. The prudent course is often to serve on both the assignor and the assignee, where there is any doubt.

Method of service

s.196, Law of Property Act 1925 applies, so service can be effected by:

- sending by registered post or recorded delivery to the tenant at their last-known place of abode, or business;

- leaving it at that address; or

- affixing it or leaving it for the tenant at the demised premises.

s.196 is not mandatory, so that service by other methods may still be effective (for example, delivering the notice to the tenant's registered office in accordance with the *Companies Act, s.1139*). However, compliance with *s.196* gains the advantage of statutory deeming provisions and helpful caselaw:

- service is deemed to have been effected in the ordinary course of post (i.e. the next working day after posting), unless it is returned undelivered by the post office (*s.196(4)*);

- so long as the notice is eventually delivered, the deemed date of service overrides the actual date of delivery (*WX Investments v Begg [2002] EWHC 925 (Ch)*);

- notice may be served even though not brought to the attention of the addressee (*Kinch v Bullard [1998] 47 EG 140*);

- service was effected where the notice was pushed under the door and accidentally hidden by the linoleum floor covering (*Newborough v Jones [1975] Ch 90*);

- service was good when notice was posted through the property's letterbox in the knowledge that the tenant was in prison and unlikely to receive it (*Van Haarlam v Kasner Charitable Trust [1992] 36 EG 135*).

As with any sort of notice, service by multiple methods is often advisable for practical reasons, and in particular service by leaving the notice at the demised premises makes for easy and reliable proof of service by witness evidence.

Consequences of service of notice

The s.146 notice does not itself effect forfeiture (nor does it oblige the landlord to proceed to forfeiture), so the landlord must still be careful, following service of the notice, to avoid waiver of the right to forfeit until such time as forfeiture has taken place.

In *Church Commissioners for England v Nodjoumi (1986) 51 P&CR 155*, a s.146 notice was served alleging an unlawful assignment of the lease.

When forfeiture proceedings were brought subsequently, though, it was on the grounds of arrears of rent, the arrears all having fallen due before the date of the s.146 notice. It was argued that service of the s.146 notice itself amounted to a waiver of the right to forfeit in relation to the arrears, since it assumed the existence of the lease at the date it was served. The court held otherwise, saying:

> *"… the section 146 notice … was the very prerequisite of the right to forfeit, and it cannot therefore be said, in my judgment, that the service of the notice destroyed the very right that it was served for the purpose of achieving."*

That case concerned a situation which was slightly unusual, in that the forfeiture was based upon a breach of covenant other than that detailed in the s.146 notice. In the usual case, where s.146 notice and forfeiture relate to the same breach, the argument is even stronger.

Tenant's response

The tenant who has received a s.146 notice is unlikely simply to wait and see whether the landlord will actually forfeit or not. It may consider that the notice is invalid, because it believes it has not breached the terms of the lease. It may consider that the time the landlord is allowing for remedy of the breach (in the notice itself, or more likely in correspondence) is too short. It may believe that any sums alleged to be due to the landlord are not actually due. Whether or not any of those circumstances applies, it will usually be very concerned about the prospect of peaceable re-entry, and want to head it off.

It was observed in Chapter 1 that the most powerful threat to tenants contained in the possibility of forfeiture is peaceable re-entry. It may be helpful to expand on that a little. Should a landlord forfeit a lease by court proceedings, the tenant can budget for the cost, and also for the expenditure of management time. Like any litigation, it will be an unwelcome distraction at best, but it is a normal business risk.

Peaceable re-entry is a different matter. The reputational damage to the tenant from customers or clients arriving at the premises to find that the landlord has taken possession is potentially considerable. Unless and until possession can be regained, the conduct of the tenant's business is completely suspended. While the tenant may regain possession by means of an injunction, pending determination of its application for relief from forfeiture, this will entail significant expense and disruption of business in the short term.

The tenant will therefore want to know how peaceable re-entry can be avoided, and one way is to respond to the notice by immediately issuing an application for relief. The tenant need not wait until forfeiture has taken place to do this; it may make an application following service of a s.146 notice (*Pakwood Transport Ltd v 15 Beauchamp Place Ltd (1977) 36 P & CR 112*). Because an application for relief will usually support the tenant in obtaining an interim injunction restoring them to possession, once it has been issued and served the landlord will be aware that peaceable re-entry would be futile. When serving the application, the tenant may therefore ask the landlord to agree that any forfeiture will be effected only by court proceedings, and the landlord is likely to concede that. In the event that it does not, the tenant may apply for an injunction confining the landlord to forfeiture by court proceedings. Given the courts' attitude to peaceable re-entry, that is likely to be granted.

Another way of preventing peaceable re-entry is to ensure that there is at all times a person present on the premises to refuse access to the landlord.

The matters addressed under this heading are considered further in Chapter 7.

Content of notice

Identifying the breach

The notice must identify the breach sufficiently accurately that the tenant can understand what is needed to put things right, and so avoid forfeiture. The landlord need not specify the required action, just identify the breach of covenant accurately.

In cases of breach of repairing covenant, the practice is to serve the notice together with a schedule of dilapidations, which identifies the alleged disrepair in great detail.

In some instances, typically in the case of breach of alienation covenant, the landlord often does not know the precise nature of the breach. The covenant will usually prohibit a range of actions: assignment and sub-letting (except with landlord's consent, and in accordance with stipulated conditions), but also holding on trust, granting licence to occupy, and parting with or sharing possession or occupation. All the landlord knows, often, is that there is somebody in occupation who should not be there, and the basis of their occupation is unexplained.

In such cases, the notice must be drafted in the alternative, so that all potential breaches of covenant are covered. Otherwise, should it turn out, for example, that the breach of covenant was sharing occupation, but that was not included among the possible breaches set out in the s.146 notice, then any purported forfeiture in reliance upon the notice would have been invalid.

Where a s.146 notice included a reference to a non-existent covenant, it was held that the rest of the notice remained valid (*Silvester v Ostrowska [1959] 1 WLR 1060*). However, where the good parts of the s.146 notice could not be separated from the bad, it was held that the whole notice was invalid (*Guillemard v Silverthorne (1908) 99 LT 584*).

Compensation

Although *s.146* states that the notice should require the tenant to pay compensation for the breach, it has been held in *Lock v Pearce [1893] 2 Ch 271* that there is no need to do so if the landlord does not want compensation in money, or where the breach cannot be compensated for in that way. A notice which omits this requirement will still be valid.

Reasonable time for remedy of the breach

Where the breach specified in the notice is capable of being remedied, the notice must require the tenant to do so. If it is irremediable, on the other hand, a notice which omits this requirement will still be valid: *Egerton v Esplanade Hotels, London Ltd [1947] 2 All ER 88*. The distinction between breaches which are remediable and those which are irremediable is also relevant as regards the availability of relief against forfeiture, since the general principle is said to be that any breach must be remedied for relief to be available. The distinction may be one of law rather than fact, and is another area of the law of forfeiture which is confused and unsatisfactory. It will be discussed in Chapter 9, in relation to the availability of relief. The uncertainty arising from the law on this point means that the s.146 notice will generally require the tenant to remedy the breach *"insofar as it is capable of remedy"*.

In the case of a remediable breach, the landlord must allow a reasonable time for the remedying of the breach to elapse between service of the notice and the forfeiture. A purported forfeiture effected before a reasonable time has elapsed will be invalid (e.g. *Cardigan Properties Ltd v Consolidated Property Investments Ltd [1991] 07 EG 132*).

The notice need not specify what the 'reasonable time' is considered to be, and the landlord will have more flexibility to respond to events in assessing when to proceed to forfeiture if it does not. Landlords will generally not specify a time period.

What is a reasonable time depends on the circumstances. A tenant trading in breach of use covenant, for example, may be able to discontinue the unlawful use at very short notice indeed; for a retailer it may be just a matter of walking across the shop and putting the 'closed' sign on the door. On the other hand, if the breach complained of is a substantial repairing breach, putting it right is likely to involve the tenant having the premises inspected by its own building surveyor and a report prepared, then a specification of works drawn up, and a tendering exercise undertaken, and finally engaging a contractor and having the works done. The process could take a year or more.

The uncertainty inherent in assessing what is a reasonable time for remedy of the breach makes for an obvious and common ground of challenge to forfeiture, and landlords will therefore tend to err on the side of caution. While the time required to remedy the breach in practical terms is obviously the prime consideration, in cases where the landlord is tempted to conclude that the required time is very short it is worth considering the remarks of Lord Russell LJ in *Horsey Estate Ltd v Steiger [1899] 2 QB 79*, that the tenant:

> " ... *ought to have the opportunity of considering whether he can admit the breach alleged; whether it is capable of remedy; whether he ought to offer any, and, if so, what, compensation; and finally ... whether he ought or ought not promptly to apply for ... relief*"

The tenant should be given time, in short, to consider its position and take advice.

Where the breach is irremediable, on the other hand, the notice need not require the tenant to remedy the breach, and no 'reasonable time' need be allowed. However, in *Billson v Residential Apartments Ltd [1992] 1 All ER 141*, the House of Lords said that even in the case of an irremediable breach a tenant should be given a period of time, typically two weeks, to consider its options. That is in line with the approach in *Horsey Estates Ltd v Steiger* quoted above.

An illustrative example of a s.146 notice is provided in the Appendix.

Forfeiture for arrears of rent

<u>Are all the arrears reserved as rent?</u>

It is conventional for service charge, insurance premiums, default interest, landlord's legal and surveying costs and other sums due under a lease to be "*reserved as rent*". Rent in the layman's sense of the price for the accommodation, before these 'extras', will often be identified as the "*Main Rent*" or "*Principal Rent*".

The chief reason for this was the old remedy of distress for rent, which enabled the landlord to use bailiffs to recover all sums reserved as rent under a lease, without the expense and delay of going to court. Since the replacement of distress by Commercial Rent Arrears Recovery ("CRAR"), this reason has disappeared. The legislation is clear that CRAR may only be used to recover the main rent, and not any of those 'extras', whether reserved as rent or not.

There is the residual reason that in the case of non-payment of sums which are reserved as rent, the landlord can proceed to forfeiture without serving a s.146 notice. It is a small convenience, but still worth having. Before forfeiting on the ground of arrears, it should be checked whether all sums outstanding are reserved as rent. If some are not, then either the landlord should serve a s.146 notice in relation to the non-rent items before forfeiting, or it should be clear that forfeiture will be effected only in reliance upon the rent items. In the latter case, the tenant will be able to obtain relief from forfeiture by paying only the rent items, while leaving the landlord to its other remedies in respect of the non-rent items.

<u>Has the 'grace period' expired?</u>

Leases will invariably provide that the right to forfeit arises only after a specified 'grace period', that is, the rent must have been outstanding for a certain length of time. This is typically 14 days, though any shorter or longer period may be negotiated, or indeed a grace period might be dispensed with altogether, so that a right to forfeit arises immediately if payment is not made on the due day (possible, though highly unusual).

Forfeiture should not, of course, be effected until the grace period has expired. As is always the case where leases or other contracts specify time limits, some careful calculation and interpretation of the provision may be needed, and it may often be safer to leave a couple of days' margin of error.

<u>Is there any set-off available to the tenant?</u>

It is also worth considering any reasons for non-payment. A tenant which is in the middle of a cashflow difficulty, or which is simply careless of due dates, is a different proposition from a tenant which genuinely believes it has a right to withhold payment. If a tenant has a claim against the landlord in respect of which it has a right of set-off against the rent, then to the extent that the amount of the claim exceeds the amount of any instalments of rent, those instalments are not due, and non-payment of them does not give rise to a right to forfeit. Most leases contain provision prohibiting any set-off, but the wording of the clause will bear looking at carefully.

That is because there are different categories of set-off, and the landlord will want to be sure that all are excluded. Legal set-off may apply where A is owed a sum by B, but B is also owed a sum by A (*Hanak v Green [1958] 2 All ER 141*). In those circumstances, unless the right is excluded, B can set one debt against the other, and pay A the balance, or as the case may be, claim the balance from A. This will rarely apply in landlord and tenant situations, since the landlord rarely owes money to the tenant. A clause which excluded only legal set-off would therefore not assist the landlord much.

There is also equitable set-off, which will arise more commonly in relation to leases (e.g *British Anzani (Felixstowe) Ltd v International Marine Management (UK) Ltd [1980] QB 137*). This may arise where A is owed a sum by B, but B has an unliquidated claim against A arising out of the same transaction (i.e. the lease). For example, the landlord is owed £10,000 rent, but the tenant claims that the landlord's failure to repair the roof has caused him to suffer loss which he puts at £12,500. Applying equitable set-off, the tenant need not pay the rent arrears.

A further possibility is non-payment in reliance upon the common law remedy of recoupment. In *Lee-Parker v Izzet [1971] 1 WLR 1688*, a tenant carried out repair work which was the landlord's responsibility, but which the landlord had failed to do. The tenant's expenditure was to be regarded as payment for the landlord's benefit – effectively a payment on account of rent – and so it was entitled to withhold the equivalent amount from further instalments as they fell due. The judge went out of his way to emphasise that this was not the remedy of set-off, but the distinct common law remedy of recoupment.

The potential pitfalls for the landlord are illustrated by *Connaught Restaurants Limited v Indoor Leisure Ltd [1994] 1 WLR 501*. Premises in the basement of the Connaught Rooms in Great Queen Street, London, were demised to Indoor Leisure for the purposes of its business of running a snooker hall. Connaught was the landlord. In the lease, the landlord undertook repairing obligations. The tenant covenanted to pay rent "*without any deduction*".

The landlord breached its repairing obligations. Water frequently entered the basement premises through the roof and through leaking pipes, rendering parts of the premises unusable. The tenant stopped paying its rent, claiming it had suffered substantial damages as a result of disruption to its business, and was entitled to a set-off against the rent.

The trial judge had concluded that the words "*without any deduction*" meant that set-off was excluded. The Court of Appeal recognised that it was possible to exclude the right of equitable set-off, but held that this could only occur as a result of clear language: see *Modern Engineering (Bristol) Ltd v Gilbert- Ash (Northern) Ltd [1974] AC 689*. The Court considered that the words "*without any deduction*" were insufficiently clear to achieve that.

Ideally, the landlord will wish the lease to exclude equitable set-off expressly, as well as legal set-off and any other deduction of any nature whatsoever. Most modern leases will have wide clauses of this sort, but the practice is not uniform, and the position should always be checked.

Is formal demand required?

At common law, the rule is that a landlord cannot forfeit for non-payment of rent unless the rent has been formally demanded. (This rule may have a familiar sound to habitual players of the board game 'Monopoly'). Leases invariably exclude the rule (see the example for-feiture clause in Chapter 2), and where it is excluded, the landlord may forfeit even where the tenant has received no invoice for the rent: *Railtrack plc v Ohajah [2000] EGCS 88*.

Very unusually, a lease which does not dispense with formal demand may be encountered. In such a case, the common law requirements for a demand apply:

- It must be made by the landlord or his authorised agent;

- It must be made on (not before or after) the final day of the grace period;

- It must be made before sunset on that day;

- It must be made at the proper place, which is either the place for payment specified in the lease, or if there is none then the demised premises; and

- It must be made for the then current and outstanding quarterly amount, not any previously accrued arrears.

However, there are a couple of statutory exceptions, in cases where the landlord proceeds by court action, not by peaceable re-entry:

Under the *County Courts Act 1984, s.139(1)*, service of a claim form in the County Court constitutes a demand for this purpose, so long as: the rent is over six months in arrear; the landlord has a right to forfeit for non-payment of rent; and there are insufficient goods on the premises to recover payment by means of Commercial Rent Arrears Recovery.

Under the *Common Law Procedure Act 1852, s.210*, equivalent provision is made in relation to the High Court.

While the landlord may gratefully take advantage of those provisions, it does mean that it will effectively be impossible to forfeit by peaceable re-entry, which is often the preferred way of proceeding when forfeiting for non-payment of rent.

Forfeiture for breach of repairing obligation

Dealing with breach of tenant's repairing obligation before the end of the term presents a variety of difficulties. Specific performance of a tenant's repairing obligation is hardly ever granted, since it is very difficult to define with sufficient precision what work is required, and the upshot would probably be the parties having to return to court for further guidance repeatedly, effectively requiring the court to supervise the works. Specific performance was granted in *Rainbow Estates Ltd v Tokenhold [1999] Ch 64*, although the judge emphasised that it was an exceptional case. *Blue Manchester Ltd v North West Ground Rents Ltd [2019] EWHC 142 (TCC)* is a more recent example, though that was in relation to a landlord's repairing obligation, and in practice the courts appear slightly more inclined to assist tenants in this way than they do landlords. What the two cases have in common is that there was no other real remedy available.

Probably the most useful remedy for the landlord in mid-term is the so-called 'self-help' remedy, otherwise known as a Jervis v Harris claim, following *Jervis v Harris [1996] Ch 195*. Most leases contain the provisions necessary to make this remedy available; it involves the landlord serving a repair notice and, in default of the tenant tackling the itemised disrepair within a specified time-frame, entering the premises to do the work itself, and then subsequently recovering the cost from the tenant as a debt claim. This procedure is not problem-free either, but the restrictions imposed on forfeiture and damages claims by the *Leasehold Property (Repairs) Act 1938* may leave it as the only effective course of action.

The *Leasehold Property (Repairs) Act 1938* was enacted to deter landlords from pursuing tenants for minor disrepair. The purpose of the Act has been judicially identified as preventing speculators from buying up a reversionary interest cheaply, forfeiting the lease for some minor disrepair, and thereby getting the property with vacant possession at well below the market value.

Under the Act, a landlord who wishes either to forfeit a lease or claim damages, in reliance on breach of a tenant's repairing obligation, must first serve a s.146 notice (of course that is a prerequisite of forfeiture anyway, but in this instance it is required before a damages claim as well). The notice must contain specified wording to bring to the tenant's attention its rights under the 1938 Act, which must be no less prominent than the other wording of the notice.

The tenant then has 28 days in which to serve a simple counternotice, claiming the benefit of the Act – this is a very simple and cheap procedure and invariably a tenant will serve the counternotice. That prevents the landlord from claiming damages or forfeiting without the court's permission, and permission can only be granted on one of five statutory grounds, which are broadly directed at ensuring that the disrepair is sufficiently significant. Those grounds are:

- That the immediate remedying of the breach is requisite for preventing substantial diminution in the value of the landlord's reversion, or that the value thereof has already been substantially diminished by the breach

- That the immediate remedying of the breach is required for giving effect in relation to the premises to the purposes of any enactment, or of any byelaw or other provision having effect under an enactment, or for giving effect to any order of the court or requirement of any authority under any such enactment or any such byelaw or other provision as aforesaid

- Where the lessee is not in occupation of the whole of the premises as respects which the covenant or agreement is proposed to be enforced, that the immediate remedying of the breach is required in the interests of the occupier of those premises or of part thereof

- That the breach can be immediately remedied at an expense that is relatively small in comparison with the much greater expense that would probably be occasioned by postponement of the necessary work

- Special circumstances exist which in the opinion of the court render it just and equitable that leave should be given

It used to be thought that on an application for permission under the Act the landlord need only make a *prima facie* case that one of the five grounds was satisfied, and that full proof of the statutory ground would wait until the trial of the substantive claim. That practice prevailed until *Associated British Ports v CH Bailey [1990] 2 AC 704*, where it was held that a ground must be established on the normal civil standard of proof, hence an application is likely to have to go to a full trial. This is an effective deterrent, since it means that enforcing the repairing obligation requires not one but two trials. That means double the expense, double the delay, and double the uncertainty and litigation risk. Applications under the Act are unusual.

The Act applies to tenancies granted for seven years or more, so long as there are three or more years of the term remaining. Therefore, it has been usual for landlords to wait to deal with disrepair until the last three years of the lease, and typically at the end of the lease. The average length of lease being granted currently is around five years, and so there are many new leases to which the Act does not apply.

The 1938 Act is not the only factor which makes it unusual for land-lords to forfeit for disrepair. It has been suggested previously that although disrepair is a continuing breach of covenant, and the right to forfeit cannot be lost by waiver, nevertheless the landlord might find it a serious inconvenience if any act of waiver required the service of a second s.146 notice, and another 'reasonable time' to elapse. As we have seen, there is Court of Appeal authority (*Farimani v Gates [1984] 2 EGLR 66*), suggesting that that may be necessary, so even in the case of forfeiture for disrepair the landlord may take precautions so as to avoid waiver, principally not accepting any rent. Where serious disrepair is involved, it may be necessary to forego rent for a significant period.

It should also be borne in mind that as in any forfeiture, it is possible that the tenant will accept the forfeiture, and leave the landlord with a vacant property. In the case of disrepair, that means that on top of all the vacant property headaches, the landlord still has a property which is in disrepair, and may require expenditure in order to re-let.

A landlord may consider forfeiture for disrepair despite these factors, but this tends to be in circumstances where the disrepair is serious and long-standing, the tenant shows little sign of being able or willing to put it right, and the remainder of the term is lengthy.

Finally, it may be noted that under *s.147, Law of Property Act 1925*, fol-lowing service by the landlord of a notice requiring the tenant to carry out purely internal decorative repairs, the court has a specific juris-diction to relieve the tenant from liability for those works if the notice is found to have been unreasonable. The notice referred to could be a s.146 notice, or perhaps a simple contractual notice to repair. This is not simply a power to relieve from forfeiture, but enables the court to relieve the tenant from the need to carry out the work at all. An early application under *s.147* could potentially therefore prevent a forfeiture. In practice, applications under *s.147* are rare, though: the 1938 Act, where it applies, would make it difficult to forfeit a lease for purely internal decorative disrepair anyway; and any landlord's claim for internal decorative disrepair is almost always just part of a wider dilap-idations claim.

Summary

Before forfeiting a lease, service of a notice under s.146, Law of Property Act 1925 is generally required. Attention must be paid to the following principal aspects:

- Does the notice accurately identify the breach of covenant?

- On whom must it be served?

- What reasonable time, if any, should be allowed for the tenant to remedy the breach of covenant?

Tenants may respond to a s.146 notice by immediately applying for relief from forfeiture so as to head off forfeiture by peaceable re-entry.

Where forfeiture is effected in reliance on arrears of rent, while there is no requirement to serve notice under s.146, Law of Property Act 1925, there are several other matters which should be checked:

- Are there any non-rent items, in respect of which a s.146 notice is required?

- Has the relevant 'grace period' expired?

- Does the tenant have any claim against the landlord which it can set-off against the rental liability?

- Has the common-law requirement for formal demand of the rent been excluded?

Forfeiture of leases for breach of repairing obligation is relatively unusual, for a number of reasons. The chief one is that the Leasehold Property (Repairs) Act 1938 requires the landlord to obtain the court's permission before commencing forfeiture, and this requires a full trial to establish one of five statutory grounds.

CHAPTER SIX
FORFEITURE BY MEANS OF
COURT PROCEEDINGS

This chapter considers one of the two methods of effecting forfeiture, namely bringing court proceedings claiming possession. It addresses the provisional nature of this type of forfeiture, and the complications of navigating the 'twilight period'. It also deals with additional relief which landlords may claim in such proceedings.

Methods of forfeiture

Having avoided waiving the right to forfeit, and complied with all required formalities, the landlord can proceed with the actual forfeiture itself. To forfeit the lease, the landlord must do something which demonstrates an unequivocal intention to bring the lease to an end. There are two ways of doing that: (a) peaceable re-entry, and (b) serving proceedings claiming possession.

Peaceable re-entry, which will be considered in Chapter 7, carries with it the risk of committing certain criminal offences. They represent the only restrictions on the choice between the two methods of forfeiture: so long as circumstances permit the landlord to exercise peaceable re-entry without falling foul of the criminal law, the choice is completely unrestricted, regardless of the nature of the breach of covenant. It is almost a matter of style.

However, it is suggested that if there are factual disputes requiring investigation and evidence, or genuine legal arguments, the matter will end up in court anyway, in which case forfeiture by court proceedings is indicated. This is particularly so since the courts have in recent years tended to frown somewhat on the practice of peaceable re-entry.

Forfeiture by court proceedings also facilitates obtaining a court declaration that there should be no grant of relief from forfeiture, which can be very useful in re-letting the premises (see Chapter 10). This is unlikely to be a major factor in the choice, though.

Forfeiture by service of proceedings

The theoretical basis of forfeiture by court proceedings is, as Lord Templeman observed in *Billson v Residential Apartments Ltd [1992] 1 All ER 141*, that:

> "*The bringing of an action to recover possession is equivalent to an entry for the forfeiture*".

It was held in *Canas Property Co Ltd v KL Television Services Ltd [1970] 2 QB* that forfeiture was effected by service, not simply issue, of the proceedings, because that communicated the landlord's intention to the tenant. Since the introduction of the *Civil Procedure Rules* in 1999, some have argued that it is the issue of proceedings which effects forfeiture, since *CPR 7.2(1)* provides that "*Proceedings are started when the court issues a claim form at the request of the claimant*". However, the *Canas* rule was recently affirmed in *Gibbs v Lakeside Developments Ltd [2018] EWCA Civ 2874*.

This means that efforts to avoid waiver of the right to forfeit cannot safely be relaxed until it is known that proceedings have been served. Landlords may prefer to have certainty over this by opting to serve proceedings themselves once issued, rather than leaving it to the court.

Unequivocal election to determine the lease

In order to effect forfeiture, the proceedings must evince an unequivocal intention to terminate the lease: in *Moore v Ullcoats Mining Co Ltd [1908] 1 Ch 575*, the landlord's intention was held to be equivocal, because the proceedings claimed both possession and also an injunction to enforce the tenant's covenants in the lease.

In *Wheeler v Keeble (1914) Ltd [1920] 1 Ch 57*, where claims for possession and an injunction were similarly combined, the court held that the proceedings did amount to an unequivocal election to terminate, on the basis that the claim for an injunction was ancillary to the possession claim. However, in *Calabar Properties Ltd v Seagull Autos Ltd [1969] 1 Ch 451*, *Wheeler v Keeble* was distinguished on the grounds that the claim for injunctions was expressed to be "*without prejudice to the claim for possession*", which the judge considered made it clear that they were not ancillary to the possession claim. Accordingly the proceedings were equivocal, and there had been no forfeiture.

The distinction between 'ancillary' and 'non-ancillary' injunction claims is not very satisfactory, and it is clearly safest, when claiming possession on the grounds of forfeiture, to avoid combining the claim with arguably inconsistent injunction claims. Not only would combining claims in this way very likely fail to effect forfeiture, but it would probably also waive the right to forfeit, as the injunction claim would appear to assume the continuing existence of the lease at the date of issue (*Iperion Investments Corporation v Broadwalk House Residents Ltd [1992] 2 EGLR 235*). The landlord would therefore not be able to put things right, for example by serving amended or completely new proceedings.

Registration of the action

Once issued, the claim falls within the definition of a pending land action under *s.17(1), Land Charges Act 1972* (see *Selim Ltd v Bickenhall Engineering Ltd [1981] 3 All ER 210*), and may therefore be registered under *s.5(1)a)* of that Act. In the case of registered land, the action may be protected by entry of a notice (*s.34* and *s.87(1)(a), Land Registration Act 2002*).

Effect of service

Once proceedings have been served, the choice to forfeit is generally irrevocable, and the lease cannot be restored by, for example, the landlord amending its statement of case so as to remove the claim for possession (*GS Fashions v B&Q Plc [1995] 4 All ER 899*).

Though it is logical that it is service of the proceedings which constitutes an unequivocal election to forfeit, and which therefore effects forfeiture, it is nevertheless a curiosity. That, of course, is just the beginning of the litigation process, and the parties may not get to find out what a judge thinks of it all until months later, perhaps over a year. The status of the lease will ultimately depend on the outcome of the proceedings.

(a) The landlord's claim might be dismissed, either because the court considers there was no breach of covenant, or the landlord has waived the right to forfeit, or there was a defect as regards the drafting of the s.146 notice, or the landlord did not allow a reasonable time for remedy of the breach before proceeding to forfeiture. Should the claim be dismissed, the lease has in theory never been forfeited (*Liverpool Properties Ltd v Oldbridge Investments Ltd [1985] 2 EGLR 111*).

(b) The judge may conclude that the landlord was entitled to forfeit the lease and did so correctly, but may nevertheless grant relief from forfeiture in the form of reinstatement of the lease. If so, the reinstatement is retrospective to the date of service (*Meadows v Clerical, Medical and General Life Assurance Society [1981] Ch 70*).

(c) If the court upholds the forfeiture and refuses relief, so that the outcome is an order for possession, then the lease is forfeit as of the date of service (*Elliott v Boynton [1924] 1 Ch 236*).

It is thus a provisional forfeiture which results from the service of proceedings, only to be converted to a final forfeiture in eventuality (c).

The effect of forfeiture is to bring to an end not just the lease, but any derivative interests such as sub-leases or mortgages granted out of it (*Great Western Railway Co v Smith (1876) 2 Ch D 235*). There are two statutory exceptions: the *Rent Act 1977, s.137*, and the *Housing Act 1988, s.18*, provide protection for any lawful sub-tenants under those Acts whose immediate landlords hold leases that are forfeited.

The 'twilight period'

The period from the date of service to the date of the court's order was referred to by Sir Robert Megarry V-C in *Meadows v Clerical, Medical and General* as the "*twilight period*", and this picturesque expression has been generally adopted.

The status of the lease during this period is uncertain. The landlord's position is that it has been terminated; the tenant's is that it will ultimately be found never to have been forfeited at all. That conflict raises difficult issues as to how the rights and obligations of the parties are to be treated during the twilight period.

The way in which the common law develops means that there can never be any occasion or opportunity for a judge to sit down with a blank piece of paper and draw up a set of consistent and comprehensive rules for how the property is to be managed during that period. Instead, caselaw throws up a miscellany of specific questions which the judges answer on a case-by-case basis.

- In *Driscoll v Church Commissioners for England [1957] 1 QB 330*, the issue and service of forfeiture proceedings did not prevent the tenant from applying to the Lands Tribunal under *s.84, Law of Property Act 1925* for the modification of certain covenants contained in the leases. While the landlord argued that there were no subsisting covenants to be modified, the court held that the covenants were "*potentially good*".

- *Associated Deliveries v Harrison (1984) 2 EGLR 76* confirmed that the landlord cannot enforce the tenant covenants in the lease, having unequivocally elected to terminate it. It is effectively estopped from treating the covenants in the lease as if they still subsisted. Consistently with that, the landlord is not entitled to payment of rent during that period, though it is entitled to mesne profits (discussed below).

- However, because the covenants are "*potentially good*", and because the tenant is affected by no such estoppel, the tenant can enforce the landlord covenants in the lease. In *Peninsular Maritime v Padseal [1981] 2 EGLR 43*, the tenant obtained an injunction, during the twilight period, requiring the landlord to comply with its obligation to repair and maintain a lift.

- *Meadows v Clerical, Medical and General* established that where the landlord had obtained a judgment for forfeiture, but there was an application for relief still to be determined, *Part II* of the *Landlord and Tenant Act 1954* continued to apply to the tenancy. The tenant was therefore not prevented from applying to the court under the Act for a new tenancy.

- The landlord may not operate any rent review during the twilight period, although the court may impose conditions upon any grant of relief which would preserve the right to review: *Soteri v Psylides [1991] 2 EGLR 138*.

It may be mentioned also that whereas in the case of forfeiture by peaceable re-entry the landlord immediately becomes the owner of any tenant's fixtures (*Re Palmiero: Debtor 3666 of 1999 [1999] 3 EGLR 27*), that favourable rule does not apply to forfeiture by court proceedings. The tenant retains the right to remove tenant's fixtures from the property right up to the final order for forfeiture.

Can the landlord unilaterally restore the lease?

It has already been noted that in *GS Fashions v B&Q Plc [1995] 4 All ER 899* the landlord failed to restore the lease unilaterally by amendment of its proceedings so as to remove the claim for possession. However, the tenant was not contesting the proceedings, and had admitted the landlord's right to forfeit.

That was not the case in *Mount Cook Land Ltd v The Media Business Centre Ltd [2004] EWHC 348 (Ch)*, in which it was held that discontinuance of the proceedings by the landlord was effective to restore the lease as if it had never been forfeited. The judge appeared to accept that that would not always be the case, but the judgment leaves it slightly unclear whether the landlord's claim would have to be "*indisputable*" or merely "*undisputed*" for a different result to follow. The two are perhaps conflated in his observation that in giving notice of discontinuance in this case the landlord:

> "… *was effectively conceding that it was not going to establish grounds for forfeiture*".

It is apparent from the judgment, though, that the landlord's real reason for discontinuing its claim was not a reconsideration of the merits, but to take advantage of a rent review, subsequent to the date of service of the proceedings, which had more than doubled the rent, increasing it to over £1m per annum.

Hynes v Twinsectra [1995] 71 P&CR 145 is an example of dismissal of the landlord's forfeiture claim restoring the lease as if had never been forfeited. That reflects a conventional understanding of the law, but the distinctive feature of the case is that the dismissal was by consent, despite which the landlord later argued unsuccessfully that service of the proceedings had effected forfeiture regardless.

The judge in *Mount Cook* saw no distinction between dismissal by consent on the one hand, and discontinuance on the other. However, Aldous J in *Hynes v Twinsectra* remarked that:

> "… *service of proceedings for possession is an election by the lessor to treat the lease as forfeited. Further, it is be taken as notional re-entry and thus forfeiture; but the act of forfeiture is subject to determination by the court of the validity of the claim.*"

It is arguable that while a discontinuance is not a 'determination by the court', a dismissal is, even one made by consent.

In *Ivory Gate Ltd v Spetale [1998] 2 EGLR 43*, service of forfeiture proceedings was ultimately followed by a compromise whereby the lease was transferred to the landlord, thus effecting a surrender, and the landlord then discontinued its claim. The landlord was held to be entitled to payment of the rent from the guarantors of the tenant's covenants up to the date of the compromise, and this case was relied upon in *Mount Cook* for the proposition that service of the proceedings alone does not effect forfeiture. In this instance, though, was that there was never any 'determination by the court' of the forfeiture claim, and therefore the lease remained potentially good up to the point when it was surrendered by transfer to the landlord. The discontinuance was subsequent to the surrender.

It is not particularly easy to pick the bones out of these cases, but it may be remarked that both *Hynes v Twinsectra* and *Ivory Gate Ltd v Spetale* are instances of the court upholding agreed compromises of forfeiture proceedings. *GS Fashions* and *Mount Cook*, on the other hand, are examples of landlords seeking to resile from the consequences of forfeiture unilaterally: unsuccessfully in the former, and successfully in the latter.

At any rate, the *Mount Cook Land* case is authority for the proposition that where the landlord's right to forfeit is disputed, the landlord may unilaterally restore the lease by discontinuance of its claim. That depends upon whether the tenant chooses to dispute the claim, however, and it is worth repeating the point which has been made in another chapter: if the landlord anticipates that the tenant will apply for relief, and will therefore put right all breaches of covenant in order to obtain it, that cannot be counted on. The tenant may omit to defend the proceedings, or apply for relief, and leave the premises vacant, with any breaches still not remedied.

Court rules

The court rules applicable to the claim are contained in *Civil Procedure Rules, Part 55*, and the accompanying practice direction *PD 55A*. Claims will generally be brought in the County Court, and dealt with in the County Court hearing centre serving the area where the property is situated. The Possession Claims Online facility does not apply to forfeiture claims.

Sub-tenants and mortgagees

Among other procedural requirements, under *PD 55A, r.55.4, para 2.4*, where the property is a residential one the landlord must give particulars of any sub-tenant or mortgagee, who might be entitled to claim relief against forfeiture, and the claim form must be served on them as well as the tenant, so that they have opportunity to claim relief against forfeiture. Thus, although the s.146 notice need not be served on those persons, they will be informed of the forfeiture at this stage, and be able to take action to protect their interests.

That requirement does not apply in the case of non-residential property, although in the old *Rules of the Supreme Court, Ord.6, r.2(1) (c)(iii) and (2)*, and *County Court Rules, Ord.6, r.3(1)(f) and (2)*, it was a requirement in *all* cases of forfeiture by court proceedings. Given that there is no requirement for the landlord to serve a s.146 notice on such parties, the restricted application of this requirement in the current court rules is a serious weakness in the law.

In practice, if the landlord wishes to prepare for subsequent re-letting by obtaining a declaration from the court that there should be no grant of relief, it will be useful to have served proceedings on all potential relief applicants, so that the court can be satisfied that they have had opportunity to protect their interests.

Interim payments

Under *CPR 25.7(1)(d)(ii)*, in a claim for possession of land the court may make an order for interim payment of mesne profits (see below) where it is satisfied:

"... *that, if the case went to trial, the defendant would be held liable (even if the claim for possession fails) to pay the claimant a sum of money for the defendant's occupation and use of the land while the claim for possession was pending".*

The order may specify a sum to be paid on each of forthcoming quarter days, effectively replicating the rental liability. This may be very useful, if an arrangement cannot be reached by agreement with the tenant, to preserve income flow from the property. It should be remembered, though, that whether paid by agreement or pursuant to a court order, mesne profits is not rent, and VAT cannot be charged, nor should invoices be raised.

Summary judgment

While it is open to the landlord to apply for summary judgment under *CPR 24*, on the basis that the defendant has no real prospect of success-fully defending the claim, this should rarely be successful. In *Liverpool Properties Ltd v Oldbridge Investments Ltd [1985] 2 EGLR 111*, the Court of Appeal upheld the dismissal of a summary judgment applic-ation on the basis that an application for relief is an equitable defence to the claim for forfeiture, and inextricably linked to the claim for pos-session. So long as genuine and arguable, it amounts to a defence which precludes the making of an order for possession on a summary judgment application. As regards what amounts to a genuine and arguable relief application, in *Sambrin Investments Ltd v Taborn [1990] 1 EGLR 61*, the court considered that the discretion to grant relief was so wide that:

> *"... it will be a fairly rare case where the court will be able to say that a genuine claim for relief from forfeiture is bound to fail".*

Therefore, the fact that tenant has applied for relief should usually be enough to prevent summary judgment.

Other relief claimed

The tenant does not benefit from any apportionment of rent, by reason of the forfeiture taking effect before the end of a quarter (*Capital &*

City Holdings Ltd v Dean Warburg [1989] 1 EGLR 90). Take an instance where a claim was served on 10 April, based upon non-payment of the March quarter's rent:

- The period from and including the March quarter-day up to and including the day of service of the proceedings was 17 days. The full rent for the entire March quarter (91 days) was due on 25 March, and the tenant was liable for the full amount.

- The landlord's claim would of course include that quarter's rent, if unpaid. From the end of that quarter on 23 June, though, the landlord would have no entitlement to rent, having terminated the lease. The claim should therefore seek mesne profits from 24 June *"until possession be delivered up"*, together with interest.

Mesne profits is a measure of damages in trespass, which can be claimed even where the landlord would not have re-let or occupied the property during the period of the trespass. The measure of damages is ordinarily the open market rental value (*Swordheath Properties Ltd v Tabet [1979] 1 All ER 240*). It is open to the landlord to justify a higher figure (*Clifton Securities v Huntley [1948] 2 All ER 283*), though proving a different rate would require expert valuation evidence.

The landlord may elect, instead of claiming compensatory damages, to claim restitution of the benefit received by the occupier. For example, if the occupier was paying a concessionary rent before the termination of the lease, the value of what it has received after termination is greater than the concessionary rate (*Ministry of Defence v Ashman; Ministry of Defence v Thompson [1993] 2 EGLR 107*). In many cases, there will be no difference between the compensatory and restitutionary bases of assessment (*Dean & Chapter of Canterbury Cathedral v Whitbread [1995] 1 EGLR 82*). However, there have been cases where mesne profits has been assessed as a percentage of capital value, or by reference to a rate of return on diminution in capital value (*Ramzan v Brookwide [2012] 1 All ER 903*). The latter case is a useful modern reference on damages for trespass.

It is convenient and usual, though, and the almost invariable practice, for mesne profits to be claimed at the rate of the rent payable immediately prior to forfeiture. It is rarely worth the expense of proving some other measure, and claiming at the rate of the old rent has the convenience of allowing default judgment to be entered for a liquidated sum calculated at that rate, should the opportunity arise.

It is also worth the landlord asking the court for a declaration that there should be no grant of relief from forfeiture. The proceedings should have been served on all persons entitled to claim, and so if they have chosen to take no part in the action, there is no good reason why a court would refuse this. In practice it is often sought and obtained. This makes subsequent re-letting considerably less uncertain (see Chapter 10).

An illustrative example of a Particulars of Claim is provided in the Appendix.

Summary

Service of court proceedings claiming possession is one of the two methods of forfeiting leases, the service of the proceedings being regarded as equivalent to a re-entry. The election to forfeit made in this way must be unequivocal, so that a claim for forfeiture may not be combined with a claim for an injunction to enforce performance of the tenant's covenants in the lease.

Forfeiture effected in this way must be provisional, though, since the final outcome will depend on the court's decision at the conclusion of the litigation process. During the period that the outcome is uncertain, known as the 'twilight period', the management of the property is complicated by the fact that the landlord is estopped from relying upon the terms of the lease, while the tenant is not, since the lease is potentially good until such time as the court has made its decision.

The election to forfeit by serving the proceedings is generally irrevocable, however it may be that where the tenant has contested the landlord's right to forfeit, the landlord can restore the lease by discontinuance of its claim.

Proceedings must be served on all persons entitled to apply for relief from forfeiture, to enable them to act to protect their interests.

The landlord will often combine other claims with the possession claim:

- any outstanding arrears;

- mesne profits while the occupation by the tenant continues; and

- a declaration that there should be no grant of relief from forfeiture.

CHAPTER SEVEN
FORFEITURE WITHOUT
GOING TO COURT

This chapter covers how a lease may be forfeited without the necessity of going to court to obtain an order for possession. Practicalities such as dealing with tenant's goods, and use of bailiffs are covered, along with the avoidance of potential criminal liability.

In the previous chapter we addressed how forfeiture may be effected through court proceedings. In the House of Lords' decision in *Billson v Residential Apartments Ltd [1992] 1 All ER 141*, Lord Templeman referred to that as:

> "*the civilised method of determining the lease by issuing and serving a writ*"

contrasting it with:

> "*the dubious and dangerous method of determining the lease by re-entering the premises*".

It is to dubious and dangerous matters that we now turn.

A "sure recipe for violence"?

'Peaceable re-entry', as it is conventionally called, involves securing the property physically, without going to court. Lord Templeman's remarks just quoted give a good flavour of the judicial attitude to this process. Elsewhere in his speech, he observed that the landlord had "*conceived and carried out a dawn raid which fortunately did not result in bloodshed*". In the Court of Appeal decision (reported at *[1991] 3 All ER 265*), Nicholls LJ had given his view at greater length:

"Nor can it be right to encourage law-abiding citizens to embark on a course which is a sure recipe for violence. If a landlord enters business premises without warning out of business hours, violence is all too likely when the tenant arrives the next day to reopen his shop or offices and finds he is barred from entry. The policy of the law is to discourage self-help when confrontation and a breach of the peace are likely to follow. If a tenant who is in breach of covenant will not quit but persists in carrying on his business despite the landlord's right of re-entry, the proper course for a responsible landlord is to invoke the due process of law and seek an order for possession from the court."

It is understandable that their Lordships should apprehend confrontation, but experience suggests that violence results very rarely. This is principally because the law requires, in effect, that the re-entry should indeed be 'peaceable', and in practice this means that when a property is repossessed in this way it seldom happens that both landlord and tenant (or their respective agents) are present at the premises at the same time.

Human rights

There have also been concerns over whether the remedy of peaceable re-entry is compatible with human rights.

- Under *Article 6(1)* of the *European Convention on Human Rights*: *"In the determination of his civil rights and obligations … everyone is entitled to a fair and public hearing … by an independent and impartial tribunal established by law"*. Extra-judicial remedies such as this will naturally prompt suggestions of a conflict with *Article 6*. However, since a tenant has the ability to claim relief from forfeiture, or damages in the event of the landlord unlawfully taking possession (e.g. *South Tottenham Land Securities v R & A Millett (Shops) [1983] 2 EGLR 122*), it is doubtful whether it can fairly be said that peaceable re-entry deprives the tenant of the opportunity of a hearing.

- *Article 8* provides that *"Everyone has the right to respect for his private life [and] his home"*, and it has been held that this may extend to business premises. *Article 8* rights are qualified in a number of respects, though, and a landlord would no doubt argue that exercise of the right of peaceable re-entry in relation to purely commercial premises was (a) within the law, (b) in pursuance of the legitimate aim of procuring compliance with the tenant's contractual obligations, and also (c) necessary and proportionate.

• *Article 1* of the *First Protocol*, finally, states that "*Every natural or legal person is entitled to the peaceful enjoyment of his possessions*". This Article is designed principally to protect individuals against actions of the state; the process of forfeiture, should the tenant exercise its right to seek relief, involves the court balancing the tenant's occupational rights against the landlord's right to have the lease terms complied with, and it is difficult to see how this could be considered abusive state action so as to engage the Article.

There has, at any rate, been no challenge as yet to peaceable re-entry on the basis of human rights, although in *Patel v Pirabakaran [2006] 4 All ER 506*, Wilson LJ in the Court of Appeal considered *Article 8* in relation to the prohibition on re-entry of residential premises contained in *s.2, Protection from Eviction Act 1977*. The issue was whether the prohibition extended to mixed-use premises, and he concluded that:

> "*an interpretation of section 2 of the 1977 Act that prohibits a landlord from exercising – otherwise than by proceedings in court – an alleged right of re-entry upon premises let for use as a dwelling as well as for business purposes is an interpretation that would be compatible with the tenant's rights under Article 8; and … the opposite interpretation of it would be incompatible with them.*"

Public relations

Peaceable re-entry is a procedure which continues to be controversial, and some landlords who are especially sensitive to public opinion (for example, local authority landlords) simply will not use it, except where premises have unarguably been abandoned. Other landlords are entirely unembarrassed about it. Tenants are not without protections under the law, and it is, when all is said and done, a long-established right whose legality was described by Lord Denning MR in *McPhail v Persons Unknown [1973] 1 Ch 447* as *"beyond question"*. For many landlords, any qualms or reservations they have about peaceable re-entry may be outweighed by other considerations, on a case-by-case basis, in the light of the specific circumstances.

It was suggested in the previous chapter that use of peaceable re-entry is unlikely to be helpful in a case where the nature of the dispute makes it probable that the parties will in any event find themselves in court. On the other hand, where the tenant has failed to pay some rent, because of financial problems or poor discipline, rather than from any claim to be entitled to do so, peaceable re-entry is usually quicker, cheaper and more effective than court proceedings, and landlords may feel better able to withstand any critical comment on their choice of remedy.

Methods of peaceable re-entry

Actual physical recovery of possession is not necessarily required to effect peaceable re-entry; the grant of a new lease of the premises to a third party might take effect as a forfeiture (*Redleaf Investments Ltd v Talbot (1994) The Times, 5 May*), as might re-letting the premises to an existing sub-tenant who remains in occupation (*Ashton v Sobelman [1987] 1 WLR 177*). In the latter case, however, it was held that allowing the sub-tenant to remain in occupation upon the terms of the pre-existing sub-lease was inconsistent with termination by forfeiture. To effect forfeiture in this way, there must be a grant of a new lease. It seems that whether the terms are similar, or even identical, to those of the former sub-lease need not matter. Whenever forfeiture is effected by granting a new lease, it is probably sensible to recite this in the new lease, for clarity.

The landlord must do something which shows an unequivocal intention to terminate the lease and recover possession (*Hone v Daejan Properties [1976] 2 EGLR 110*), and in the usual case there will be some physical act of taking possession. This is usually a matter of changing the locks. The forfeiture clause will usually provide that the landlord can *"re-enter part in the name of the whole"*, so that a landlord recovering possession of a 10-hectare factory site, for example, might do so by changing the lock on the main entrance to the principal site building, rather than having to change every lock on the site.

Occasionally, the property to be recovered may be an open site, where there are no locks to change. The landlord must still do something to demonstrate recovery of possession, but what that may be will depend on the circumstances. It may be as simple as posting notices around the site boundary, chaining up a gate, or stringing a chain across what would otherwise be open access. Excavating a trench around the boundary or erecting bollards could be other possibilities.

Simply securing the premises is not in itself proof of an unequivocal intention to bring the lease to an end; there must be an actual intention to terminate the lease. In *Relvok Properties Ltd v Dixon (1972) 25 P&CR 1*, a tenant had vacated premises with no intention of returning. The landlord changed the locks, but this did not amount to a forfeiture so as to prevent them claiming subsequent instalments of rent from the tenant, because it was done with the intention of protecting the security of the property. Because that case was about rent and not about possession, it was argued 'the wrong way round': the tenant seeking to establish that the landlord had forfeited, and the landlord denying it. Usually the landlord's intention is plain enough. Landlords will typically post a notice on the premises stating that they have recovered possession, to remove any potential for doubt.

Criminal restrictions

The ability to forfeit by peaceable re-entry is circumscribed by two criminal offences.

- *s.2, Protection from Eviction Act 1977* makes it a criminal offence to terminate a lease by peaceable re-entry if the premises are *"let as a dwelling"*. It was formerly thought that committing this offence could be avoided as regards mixed-use premises, by making use of the ability to re-enter part in the name of the whole. Take for instance a shop with a flat above, both let on the same lease, the flat having separate access. If the landlord were to change the locks on the commercial part of the premises, which were not let as a dwelling, then that would effect forfeiture. The lease would be terminated, as a matter of law, and removed from the title. So long as the flat, its contents and occupiers remained undisturbed, then no offence would have been committed, and the landlord could obtain an order for possession in relation to the flat at its leisure. *Pulleng v Curran (1980) 44 P&CR 58* gave support to that, holding that cessation of business use of the shop did not bring the tenancy within the *Rent Act 1977*, as a tenancy of premises *"let as a dwelling"*.

That idea was rejected in *Patel v Pirabakaran [2006] 4 All ER 506*. If the premises have both commercial and residential elements, the prohibition on peaceable re-entry extends to the commercial part too. The resulting position has at least the merit of simplicity: if there is any part of the premises which is residential, peaceable re-entry is out of the question.

• In addition, *s.6, Criminal Law Act 1977* makes it an offence for a landlord to use violence against the person or property in recovering possession of any premises, not just residential ones, so long as there is a person present on the premises who is opposed to the landlord recovering possession.

What amounts to 'violence' for this purpose, will depend on all the circumstances of an individual case. There is little caselaw to assist. Breaking open a door (*Hemmings v Stoke Poges Golf Club [1920] 1 KB 720*) probably amounts to violence, but breaking a small window to get in, picking locks or slipping them open with a credit card, or removing padlocks or bars (*Williams v Taperell (1892) 8 TLR 241*) may not be. In *Razzaq v Pala [1997] 38 EG 157* it was held that breaking locks was not unlawful.

In practice, the presence on the premises of a 'person opposed' means that it will not be possible to recover possession without resort to 'violence' within the meaning of *s.6*, and so peaceable re-entry is not possible.

The sum effect of these two provisions is to make it almost invariably the case that when peaceable re-entry is done it is only on purely commercial premises, and usually out of business hours, often over a weekend or early in the morning, or perhaps on a bank holiday, when it can be expected that no-one will be present.

This explains the reference in *Billson* to a "*dawn raid*". It also explains why violence rarely results. The landlord will have the locks changed at a time when nobody is there (6.00 a.m. in *Billson*). When the tenant arrives, the landlord's representatives have usually long gone, so that if the tenant breaks back in (which followed at 10.00 a.m. the same day in *Billson*), again no confrontation occurs.

Protecting against peaceable re-entry

It has previously been suggested that the tenant who anticipates forfeiture will usually be much more concerned about peaceable re-entry than about forfeiture by court proceedings. One method of forestalling peaceable re-entry is, as has been discussed, to apply for relief from forfeiture immediately upon receipt of a s.146 notice.

If the tenant is in arrears of rent, however, no s.146 notice need be served, and the landlord may simply change the locks without warning. Might a tenant issue a relief application in a rent-breach case in anticipation of the landlord effecting forfeiture? On the face of it, it is not a very attractive proposition that a tenant might default in its obligation to pay rent, and then effectively buy itself more time by applying for relief from forfeiture. *Barton, Thompson & Co Ltd v Stapling Machines Co [1966] 2 All ER 222, 224* suggests that this is not possible, Pennycuick J considering that an application for relief "*does not appear appropriate in advance of proceedings for possession or actual possession*". The case involved non-payment under a lease of industrial machines, not land, but the issue was discussed with explicit reference to the statutory provisions concerning relief against forfeiture of leases in rent-breach cases (see Chapter 8).

Another method of preventing peaceable re-entry is simply to ensure that there is always someone present on the premises to refuse admittance to the landlord and/or its bailiffs, so that *s.6, Criminal Law Act 1977* will effectively prevent peaceable re-entry. This might be done by camping out in the premises, or rather less uncomfortably, by engaging a round-the-clock security presence.

Use of bailiffs

Some landlords will have the knowledge, confidence and experience to effect peaceable re-entry themselves. Usually, though, landlords will prefer to employ bailiffs. Bailiffs generally offer peaceable re-entry as a relatively inexpensive service, and have a great deal of experience of the practicalities.

An experienced bailiff will:

- Liaise with the police beforehand

- Engage a locksmith

- Be aware of the potential for criminal liability, and know the limits of what they can do

- Post notices on the property stating that the lease has been forfeited

- Compile an inventory of any goods remaining on the premises, with supporting photographic evidence, to prevent subsequent dispute.

Effect of peaceable re-entry

While a degree of uncertainty attends the question whether service of proceedings claiming possession is effective by itself to terminate the lease, as discussed in the last chapter, there can be no doubt in relation to peaceable re-entry. There is no need to await determination by a court, nor is there anything further for the landlord to do to perfect the process. As in the case of forfeiture by proceedings, peaceable re-entry terminates derivative interests granted out of the lease (i.e. sub-leases and mortgages).

There is no 'twilight period', at least in theory, since (a) the absence of court proceedings means that there is no ultimate determination to be awaited, and (b) the former tenant has been dispossessed, so that there can be no issues over the ongoing management of the property. However, there may be a subsequent application for relief from forfeiture, and the tenant may regain possession pursuant to an injunction, so that this aspect of the law may feature in the context of peaceable re-entry too. There is at least the opportunity for the court to rule on any likely issues by attaching terms to any injunctive relief.

However, it is plain that the lease is terminated by the re-entry, and the consequences of that for the availability of relief from forfeiture were at issue in *Billson v Residential Apartments Ltd [1992] 1 All ER 141*. Under *s.146(2), Law of Property Act*, relief from forfeiture is available to a tenant in relation to a breach of covenant other than non-payment of rent *"where a lessor is proceeding, by action or otherwise, to enforce such a right of re-entry or forfeiture"*. Briefly, the point in *Billson* was whether a landlord who had peaceably re-entered could no longer be said to be *"proceeding"* to recover possession, since it had already 'proceeded'. This will be discussed more fully in Chapter 9, but for now it is sufficient to note that peaceable re-entry does not prevent a subsequent application for relief under *s.146(2)*.

As in the case of forfeiture by proceedings, peaceable re-entry in mid-quarter gives rise to no apportionment of rent in the tenant's favour,

and the tenant is liable for the entire quarter's rent falling due on the quarter-day immediately prior to the forfeiture
(*Capital & City Holdings Ltd v Dean Warburg [1989] 1 EGLR 90*).

Response to peaceable re-entry

The tenant that finds itself locked out of its premises may seek an injunction to regain access; that will entail urgently issuing a claim for relief from forfeiture, perhaps claimed in the alternative to a declaration that the forfeiture was unlawful, depending on the circumstances. A hearing at very short notice would follow, to seek an interim injunction pending the determination of the application for relief. In cases of great urgency, the interim injunction might be sought on the strength of an undertaking to issue the substantive claim forthwith, though it is always preferable to have issued beforehand.

The injunction will usually be forthcoming, though the tenant will invariably be required to give an undertaking to pay any damages suffered by the landlord as a result of the interim injunction being imposed, in the event that it is not subsequently made permanent. The tenant will also usually have to undertake to pay mesne profits during the period of its resumed occupation, typically at the rate of the rent under the lease.

The court will require to be satisfied that the application for relief has a real chance of success, though this is not likely to present a difficult hurdle in most cases, since the courts "*lean against forfeiture*", and relief is readily obtained. In theory it might be a relevant consideration if the breach were one which is considered 'irremediable' at law, since the remedy of breaches is said to be a requirement for the grant of relief. In practice, though, relief is often granted in relation to irremediable breaches. (There is further discussion of these aspects in Chapters 8 and 9).

The process may occupy one or more days of the lawyers' and the tenant's time, which will be expensive and also very disruptive of business.

Advantages of peaceable re-entry

Judicial distaste and risk of criminal liability notwithstanding, peaceable re-entry remains in widespread use. The reasons have been covered previously, but as a quick reminder:

- It is quicker and cheaper than court proceedings. When forfeiting by court proceedings, even if judgment is obtained in default, it is then necessary to issue a writ or warrant for possession, and then necessary to await enforcement by County Court bailiffs or High Court Enforcement Officers. That is all likely to take several weeks, and of course the timescale is much longer if the proceedings are defended.

- It is highly effective and, indeed, the 'ultimate security for payment of rent'. The only warning that need be given is a s.146 notice, and even that is not required in the case of arrears of rent, which is when peaceable re-entry is most likely to be used. The landlord simply turns up unannounced and takes possession, and the tenant who wants to be re-admitted has no real alternative but to pay the arrears, plus interest and costs.

- It also has the advantage that the landlord immediately becomes the owner of any items found on the premises which would otherwise have been tenant's fixtures: *Re Palmiero: Debtor 3666 of 1999 [1999] 3 EGLR 27*.

Disadvantages of peaceable re-entry

- There is potential for violent confrontation.

- There is a risk of incurring criminal liability.

- The landlord will have to deal with the various vacant property issues outlined in Chapter 3. Of those, it is worth saying more on the topic of tenant's goods left in the property. Since, in the case of a peaceable re-entry, the tenant has usually been taken by surprise, it is highly likely that the premises are full of their goods. It will not be possible to market the property until they have been cleared.

It may often be the case that the tenant owes significant amounts in rent and other sums due under the lease, and the landlord may plan to sell the goods in satisfaction of the debt. In the odd instance the landlord might be lucky enough to hold a money judgment against the tenant, which could be enforced by taking control of the goods, but otherwise there is no legal entitlement to sell them. Commercial Rent Arrears Recovery cannot be exercised after forfeiture. Selling the goods in the absence of any legal entitlement to do so would amount to the tort of conversion, and is therefore not advised (some landlords may do it anyway, but that is a commercial, practical decision, not a legal one).

The tenant will of course be invited to remove their goods, but will often not be willing to assist the landlord in this way, since it would incur storage costs (and in the meantime the landlord is storing the goods for free). As the landlord is involuntary bailee of the goods, it is often a good idea to include them in the landlord's insurance cover (any additional premium will not be recoverable from the tenant). The landlord must, as involuntary bailee, afford the tenant access to the goods at all reasonable times. The goods can be removed and taken elsewhere, so long as the tenant is told where they have been taken, and continues to have access. Any storage charges will not be recoverable from the tenant.

The landlord can dispose of the goods after serving notice under the *Torts (Interference with Goods) Act 1977*, and after a period of time *"such as will afford the bailor a reasonable opportunity of taking delivery of the goods"*. It will have to account to the tenant for the proceeds of sale.

Many modern leases include terms providing for the landlord to be able to dispose of goods following lease termination (again, usually accounting to the tenant for the proceeds of sale). Such provisions amount to a contractual, voluntary bailment. They will typically set out a timetable, (e.g. the landlord may dispose of the goods once seven days have elapsed after the lease came to an end). Some landlords' advisers feel it is prudent to serve notice under the 1977 Act as well, even if there is a contractual entitlement to deal with the goods. That may give rise to a doubt over whether the landlord must then wait a *"reasonable time"* before disposing of the goods, or can rely upon the contractual period. However, *s.12(8)* states that the 1977 Act is subject to the express terms of any contractual bailment, so it should be safe for the landlord to rely upon the contractual period.

The position appears to be that if there is no contractual provision, then the landlord can rely upon the 1977 Act. If there is a contractual framework, then its terms take precedence over what the Act provides. However, there is no harm in serving a notice under the Act as well. In either case, there is a residual common law duty to do what is *"right and reasonable"* as regards the goods: *Campbell v Redstone Mortgages Ltd [2014] EWHC 3081 (Ch)*.

Anecdotally, tenants will sometimes attend at the premises to collect their goods, and then allege that among them were items of value which are now missing, thus setting up a claim against the landlord. This is why it is useful for bailiffs to inventorise and photograph goods upon recovering possession.

One further aspect of this problem is that most businesses now use computer equipment and media of one sort or another, and among the goods found on repossessed premises there are likely to be laptops, memory sticks, hard drives, disks etc. Landlords must be careful not to interfere with those items, as any use or processing of personal data may lead to the landlord taking on responsibility as 'data controller', and incurring penalties under the *Data Protection Act 2018* and the *General Data Protection Regulation*.

Summary

Peaceable re-entry is the recovery of possession of leased premises without the necessity of going to court. While judicial disapproval has been expressed of peaceable re-entry, and there is some debate as to whether it falls foul of the Human Rights Act 1998, nevertheless many landlords will continue to use it in appropriate circumstances, usually undisputed arrears of rent. In such a case, it can be done without warning, since there is no requirement to serve a s.146 notice.

A lease of premises which includes any residential element cannot be forfeited by this method without committing a criminal offence. It is also a criminal offence to recover possession by means of violence against the person or property (thereby effectively ruling out peaceable re-entry) if there is any person present on the property opposed to the landlord doing so.

Peaceable re-entry is usually effected by bailiffs, who are familiar with the practicalities and with the criminal restrictions.

Peaceable re-entry can be very quick, cheap and effective. On the other hand, it may involve practical headaches such as dealing with tenant's goods left at the premises.

CHAPTER EIGHT
RELIEF FROM FORFEITURE –
NON-PAYMENT OF RENT

This chapter considers the availability of relief from forfeiture in cases where the reason for forfeiture was non-payment of rent. It addresses the range of available jurisdictions for the grant of relief, and the different rules applying to the grant of relief in favour of tenants, mortgagees and sub-tenants.

Relief from forfeiture can be described loosely as reinstatement of the lease, though that is only one form which it may take. It is perhaps a better description to say that a grant of relief restores the applicant to possession. This can cause complications if an application for relief is made after the landlord has let the premises to a third party, and that situation is considered in Chapter 10. An application for relief can be made by way of counterclaim in the landlord's possession proceedings or, where the landlord has effected forfeiture by peaceable re-entry, as a stand-alone application under *Civil Procedure Rules, Part 55*.

As to when an application may be made, we have mentioned previously that where a s.146 notice has been served, an application can be made immediately: *Pakwood Transport Ltd v 15 Beauchamp Place Ltd (1977) 36 P & CR 112*. There is no need to wait for the landlord actually to forfeit, and a pre-emptive application may be useful in discouraging a peaceable re-entry. As regards forfeiture based on non-payment of rent, though, no s.146 notice need be served, and *Barton, Thompson & Co Ltd v Stapling Machines Co [1966] 2 All ER 222* suggests that, in the absence of a s.146 notice, an application for relief may only be made following peaceable re-entry, or service of forfeiture proceedings.

Relief was originally granted under the court's inherent equitable jurisdiction, on the basis that since the right to forfeit secured payment of the rent, a tenant that paid the landlord all arrears, plus interest and costs, should be allowed to keep their lease.

In relation to non-rent breaches of covenant, relief from forfeiture was historically more problematic, since the general principle adopted by the courts was that relief was not available unless the landlord could be placed in the same position as if the breach had not occurred. This can be achieved as regards non-payment of rent, so long as interest and costs are paid as well as the arrears, but it is less clearly possible as regards other breaches. Over time a very limited jurisdiction emerged to relieve against forfeiture for non-rent breaches in cases where the breach had been occasioned by fraud, accident, mistake or surprise (*per* Parker J in *Matthew v Smallwood [1910] 1 Ch 777*).

There has, however, been significant statutory intervention in this area of the law. There is now a variety of jurisdictions under which the court may relieve from forfeiture, for non-payment of rent and for other breaches, with different rules applying to each. To identify which one applies, it is necessary to know four things:

- Whether the right to forfeit arises in relation to non-payment of rent, or some other breach or event;

- The method of forfeiture adopted: peaceable re-entry or court proceedings;

- Whether the application for relief is made in the High Court or the County Court (which may of course follow from the landlord's choice of forum, if forfeiture has been effected by service of court proceedings); and

- Whether the applicant for relief is the tenant, or the holder of a derivative interest: a sub-tenant or mortgagee.

Rent breach – peaceable re-entry – tenant's application

Where the tenant applies for relief following peaceable re-entry by the landlord for non-payment of rent, relief may be granted in the High Court under its inherent equitable jurisdiction (exercisable by virtue of *s.38, Senior Courts Act 1981*). The County Court, as a creature of statute, has no inherent jurisdiction as such, but *s.139(2), County Courts Act 1984* gives the County Court the same power to grant relief from forfeiture as the High Court, in cases of peaceable re-entry for non-payment of rent. To obtain relief, in either court, the tenant will be required to pay all arrears, plus interest and costs (*Gill v Lewis [1956] 2 QB 1*).

The effect of a grant of relief, in either court, will be that the tenant continues to hold the premises on all the previous terms, with no need for the grant of a new lease: *s.38(2), Senior Courts Act 1981* and *s.139(2), County Courts Act 1984*.

Application will be made under *Civil Procedure Rules, Part 55*, and can be made in either court, though it will usually be in the County Court hearing centre serving the area in which the property is situated. That is subject to the time limit in *s.139(2), County Courts Act 1984*, however. Under that provision, application to the County Court must be made within six months of the re-entry.

There is no time limit in the High Court; in *Thatcher v C H Pearce [1968] 1 WLR 748* it was said that an application must be made "*with reasonable promptitude*". The High Court often takes the six-month limit as a guide, but it may be departed from.

In *Pineport Ltd v Grangeglen Ltd [2016] EWHC 1318 (Ch)*, the issue was whether a High Court application by a tenant had been made "*with reasonable promptitude*". The tenant had paid a £90k premium for a 125-year lease of an industrial unit. Under the lease, it agreed to pay rents including £100 in ground rent, insurance premiums and service charge contributions. The lease contained the usual right to forfeit in the event that the rent should remain unpaid after the specified grace period.

After substantial arrears had built up, the landlord forfeited the lease by way of peaceable re-entry, on 24 April 2014. The tenant claimed relief, but only after a gap of 14 months, its claim being issued on 23 June 2015. No application could be made in the County Court, since more than six months had elapsed, and so the claim was brought in the High Court.

The landlord argued that a delay of 14 months was reason enough for the court to refuse relief. Steps had been taken to ensure that demands for the rent reached the tenant, and the tenant was aware that the re-entry had taken place. It also argued that the delay had caused significant prejudice by increasing its costs and expenses.

The Court said that the tenant's lengthy delay in making the application would be difficult to overcome, but that it was just one of the factors to be considered. The court took account of:

- 'Human factors' including the tenant's mental health and the effect that depression had had on his ability to make decisions or take steps to remedy the situation;

- The steps which the tenant was taking to sell his other assets, to enable him to pay the arrears and landlord's costs;

- The 'windfall' which the landlord would get if relief were refused, since the value of the lease (£275,000) was disproportionate compared to the outstanding arrears (£24,000);

- The lack of prejudice to the landlord as a result of the late payment and the delayed relief application, assuming that all arrears, interest and costs would be paid; and

- The landlord's failure to market or re-let the property.

The court decided that in the circumstances, the tenant had a sufficient explanation for the delayed application which, despite the significant delay, was made with *"reasonable promptitude"*. The court granted relief, provided that the arrears, interest and landlord's costs were paid within a specified time.

The decision should be regarded as an outlier, and not as the herald of a wave of late relief applications. Indeed, its correctness has already been doubted, in *Gibbs v Lakeside Developments [2018] EWCA Civ 2874*. Nevertheless, it demonstrates that the six-month guideline is not completely reliable where High Court applications relying upon the inherent equitable jurisdiction are concerned.

Rent breach – peaceable re-entry – application by sub-tenant/mortgagee

Who may apply

In the case of a rent breach where the landlord has peaceably re-entered, relief is available under *s.146(4), Law of Property Act 1925* to *"any person claiming as under-lessee any estate or interest in the property comprised in the lease or any part thereof"*. According to *Egerton v Jones [1939] 2 KB 702*, a mortgagee by sub-demise is an *"underlessee"* within the meaning of the sub-section, and therefore able to apply for relief. By virtue of *s.87(1), Law of Property Act 1925*, a chargee by way of legal mortgage has *"the same protection, powers and remedies"* as a mortgagee by sub-demise, and is therefore also entitled to apply for relief as if it were an underlessee (e.g. *Chelsea Estates Investment Trust Co Ltd v Marche [1955] 1 Ch 328*).

It is therefore clear that sub-tenants, mortgagees by sub-demise and chargees by way of legal mortgage can apply for relief under *s.146(4)*. Moreover, it is equally clear that the same categories of persons may apply, following peaceable re-entry in reliance upon a rent breach, under *s.139(2), County Courts Act 1984*, since any such applicant will be *"a person with an interest under a lease of the land derived (whether immediately or otherwise) from the lessee's interest therein"* (*s.138(9C)*).

The position becomes confused when one proceeds to consider other categories of chargee. A tenant may appropriate or 'charge' their lease for the payment of a sum of money or some other obligation, and where such a charge is registered, it takes effect as if it were a charge by way of a legal mortgage, even though not expressed as such, because

Land Registration Act 2002, s.132(1) defines *"charge"* widely to include *"any mortgage, charge or lien for securing money or money's worth"*. Registered charges are often referred to as 'legal charges', as distinguished from 'equitable charges'.

Typically, an equitable charge will be created by a charging order made by the court in favour of a creditor of the tenant. Confusion arises, though, from loose usage, with the terms 'equitable charge', 'legal charge', 'equitable mortgage', and 'equitable lien' often used interchangeably. There is at least a clear distinction between a mortgage, which involves the transfer of legal and equitable ownership to the creditor, and an equitable charge, which does not.

There is certainly a practical case for the availability of relief from forfeiture to extend to equitable chargees, which can be illustrated by a short example. A creditor might obtain judgment for £200,000 against its debtor, and secure the judgment debt by means of a charging order over a lease with a significant value. The lease might then be forfeited by the landlord for non-payment of arrears of rent amounting to £1,000. The tenant might lack the funds to apply for relief or pay the arrears. If the creditor were unable to apply for relief in that event, it would lose all security for enforcement of the judgment. That possibility has been judicially described as *"manifestly unjust"*, and indeed *"astonishing"*, and as raising *"a serious question mark over the value of a charging order over leases and [revealing] a serious gap in the enforcement process."*

In *Bland v Ingram's Estates Ltd [2001] 2 EGLR 23*, the Court of Appeal held that:

(a) The inherent jurisdiction to relieve against forfeiture for non-payment of rent was restricted to applications by those who are entitled to possession of the land or have a legal estate or equitable interest in it, which did not include equitable chargees.

(b) Moreover, *s.146(4)* could not assist, since an equitable chargee is not a "*person claiming as under-lessee any estate or interest in the property comprised in the lease*".

(c) However, an application under *s.139(2), County Courts Act 1984* may be made by "*a person with an interest under a lease of the land derived (whether immediately or otherwise) from the lessee's interest therein*", a description which, in *Croydon (Unique) Ltd v Wright [2001] Ch 318*, the court had considered wide enough to encompass equitable chargees.

Since the jurisdiction exercised under *s.139(2)* is co-extensive with that of the High Court, which in the case of peaceable re-entry is exercising its inherent jurisdiction, relief could not be granted directly on that basis (point *(a)* above). The court further held, though, that a chargor under an equitable charge (the tenant, for our purposes) owed an implied obligation to the chargee to take reasonable steps to preserve the chargee's security, which extended to applying for relief where the lease had been forfeited for non-payment of rent. Where the tenant did not seek relief, the equitable chargee might therefore obtain relief indirectly by making an application under *s.139(2)*, joining the tenant to the proceedings as defendant, and claiming relief in their shoes.

This 'indirect relief' solution has a slightly *ad hoc* feel about it. It has not as yet been extended to cases of forfeiture for non-rent breaches, where preservation of the chargee's security would require the taking of steps other than the payment of money. Also, since it would appear to be available only in the form of preservation of the chargee's security, it would seem that relief could only take the form of reinstatement of the forfeited lease, not the grant of a new tenancy in favour of the applicant (as to which, see below).

Procedure and time limit

Where an application for relief is made by a sub-tenant or mortgagee under *s.146(4)* or *s.139(2)*, as in the case of an application by a tenant following peaceable re-entry for a rent breach, *Part 55* of the *Civil Pro-*

cedure Rules governs the process, and the application will usually be made in the County Court hearing centre local to the property.

It has been held that the decision of the House of Lords in *Billson v Residential Apartments Ltd [1992] 1 All ER 141* as to the time for applying for relief under *s.146(2)* (dealt with in the next chapter) applies also to applications under *s.146(4)* (see *Rexhaven v Nurse [1995] EGCS 125*). That means that the court can entertain an application by a sub-tenant or mortgagee after a peaceable re-entry, but that undue delay may defeat the application. The safest course will be to make an application at the earliest opportunity.

Where application is made under *s.139(2)*, the same time limit applies as in the case of a tenant's application, namely six months from the date of the peaceable re-entry.

Nature of relief granted

Where relief is granted under *s.139(2)*, the outcome is the reinstatement of the former lease, as already stated above.

The outcome of a successful application under *s.146(4)* will be an order for the grant of a new lease to the applicant (*Cadogan v Dimovic [1984] 2 All ER 168*). In the case of an application by a mortgagee, the new lease would be held subject to the mortgagor's equity of redemption.

The court has a wide discretion as to the terms on which relief will be granted. The applicant will invariably be required to pay all arrears under the forfeited lease, together with interest (*Gray v Bonsall [1904] 1 KB 601*). The court may order that the relief applicant pay the landlord's costs (e,g. *Factors (Sundries) Ltd v Miller [1952] 2 All ER 630*), and if the applicant is a sub-tenant or mortgagee, but it was the tenant's default which led to the forfeiture, the applicant may look to recover those costs (and its own) from the tenant. That could be by way of joining the tenant to the proceedings and seeking an order to that effect, or it could be by way of a separate claim under the terms of the sub-lease, in which the tenant is likely to have covenanted with the sub-tenant to observe the terms of the head-lease.

The terms of the new lease to be granted by way of relief will of course be the key issue. The general principle of the grant of relief in this form is that a landlord should be left in no worse position than if the for-feiture had never happened (*Hill v Griffin [1987] 1 EGLR 81*). A sub-tenant may therefore have to take on terms derived from the head-lease which are more onerous than those in its sub-lease. For example, it may have had a repairing obligation limited by reference to a schedule of condition, but may find that as a consequence of obtaining relief it is required to assume a full repairing obligation.

A sub-tenant of part will not generally be forced to take a lease of more than its part by way of relief (*Chatham Empire Theatre Ltd v Ultrans Ltd [1961] 1 WLR 817*). Otherwise, a sub-tenant of a single floor of a ten-storey office building might be required to take a new lease of the entire building. The new rent to be paid under a lease of part granted by way of relief will usually be assessed proportionately, and the applicant will also usually be required to pay a proportion of the head-lease arrears.

The breadth of the court's discretion should not be lost sight of, though. If each floor of our ten-storey office building were sub-let sep-arately, and all of the ten sub-tenants were to apply for relief, the court might consider that the additional management burden of dealing with ten head-leases of part would be a hardship to the landlord, and that relief should be refused. Also, in *London Bridge Buildings Co v Thomson (1903) 89 LT 50*, a sub-tenant of part was required to pay *all* of the arrears accrued under the head-lease, not just a proportion.

Evidently, a sub-tenant or mortgagee considering an application for relief under *s.146(4)* must give careful consideration to the terms on which relief is likely to be granted; and that is not always an easy pre-diction to make. At the same time, it will be under pressure to make any relief application promptly, so as not to lose the possibility of relief altogether.

Rent breach – court proceedings – tenant's application

Where the landlord has forfeited by service of court proceedings, the tenant's claim for relief should be made by way of counterclaim under *Part 20, Civil Procedure Rules*.

High Court

To prevent hardship to landlords arising from tenants making applications for relief long after forfeiture, *s.2* of the *Landlord and Tenant Act 1730* first introduced a six-month time limit. That provision is now repealed, and *ss.210* to *212, Common Law Procedure Act 1852* apply instead. As Lord Denning MR said in *Belgravia Insurance Co Ltd v Meah [1964] 1 QB 436*:

> "*In cases of non-payment of rent, relief is still based fundamentally on the jurisdiction of Courts of Equity to grant relief, subject to the limitations imposed by sections 210 and 212 of the Common Law Procedure Act 1852*".

This inherent equitable jurisdiction, as noted above, is now exercised in the High Court by virtue of *s.38, Senior Courts Act 1981*.

Under those provisions of the 1852 Act:

- If at least six months' arrears are owing, automatic relief may be obtained if the tenant pays all arrears and costs before trial: *s.212*. The form which relief will take in those circumstances is that the landlord's action will be stayed, and the tenant will continue to hold the premises under the terms of the original lease, with no need for grant of a new lease.

- If payment is not made before trial, under *s.210* the tenant must make payment and apply for relief within six months of enforcement of the order for possession. Except in very exceptional circumstances, relief will be granted upon payment regardless of any other considerations of the conduct of the parties, or other breaches of covenant: *Gill v Lewis [1956] 2 QB 1.*

- If the arrears are less than six months, the jurisdiction for relief is the court's inherent equitable jurisdiction, exercised by virtue of *s.38, Senior Courts Act 1981* and *s.139(2), County Courts Act 1984*, as in the case of peaceable re-entry for non-payment of rent (above). The court will adopt the six-month time limit under *s.210* as a guide. Again, the tenant will invariably be required to pay all arrears, interest and costs in order to obtain relief, and *s.211* debars the tenant from relief unless it does so.

County Court

In the County Court, it is *s.138, County Courts Act 1984* which governs. The provisions are very similar to those in the 1852 Act, though there is no qualification that at least six months' arrears must be owing.

- Relief is granted automatically if all arrears, interest and costs are paid in at least five clear days before trial. This must include all mesne profits due since the commencement of the forfeiture proceedings: *Maryland Estates v Bar Joseph [1998] 27 EG 142.*

- Alternatively, the court may make a suspended order to allow payment within no less than four weeks, and if the tenant makes payment within that time it obtains relief.

- Otherwise, the tenant must apply for relief within six months of enforcement of the order for possession.

Thus, although there are some differences of detail, the position in each Court is broadly the same: relief is granted automatically if all arrears, interest and costs are paid into court before trial. Otherwise, the tenant must apply for relief within six months of enforcement of the order for possession and will be required to pay all arrears, interest and costs, in order to obtain relief.

Rent breach – court proceedings – application by sub-tenant/mortgagee

Sub-tenants' and mortgagees' applications for relief, where it is a rent breach and the landlord has forfeited by court proceedings, are governed by the same provisions as those applicable to tenants, and the outcome (if successful) is the same, namely reinstatement of the former lease.

In the High Court, under *s.210, Common Law Procedure Act 1852*, application may be made by a "*person claiming or deriving under the [tenant's] lease*", which includes sub-tenants and mortgagees. It does not include equitable chargees (*Bland v Ingram's Estates Ltd [2001] 2 EGLR 23*).

As regards the County Court, the availability of an application under *s.138, County Courts Act 1984* extends to a "*person with an interest under a lease of the land derived (whether immediately or otherwise) from the lessee's interest therein*" (*s.138(9C)*). That clearly includes sub-tenants and mortgagees, and in *Croydon (Unique) Ltd v Wright [2001] Ch 318*, the Court of Appeal held that it extends also to equitable chargees. It appears therefore that relief under *s.138* is available to an equitable chargee without any necessity for the device of 'indirect relief', discussed above.

It was held in *Hare v Elms [1893] 1 QB 604* that if a sub-tenant or mortgagee applies for relief after judgment in the landlord's action for possession, so that the lease has actually been finally determined, reinstatement of the lease would impose a liability on the former tenant. Therefore, the applicant should make the original tenant and, if the lease had been assigned, the last assignee, party to the application. Since the *Landlord and Tenant (Covenants) Act 1995*, assignment of the lease automatically releases former tenants under *s.5*, so it may be that joining former tenants would no longer be considered necessary.

There is an overlapping jurisdiction, in that the sub-tenant or mort-gagee (though not an equitable chargee, see above) might also apply for relief from forfeiture under *s.146(4), Law of Property Act 1925* at any time before the landlord has actually obtained possession pursuant to a court order. If successful, the outcome would be an order for a new lease, in the same way as if the application had been made following peaceable re-entry (above).

Summary

There is a range of jurisdictions under which relief from forfeiture may be granted, which are considered both in this chapter and in Chapter 9. This chapter is concerned with relief from forfeiture for non-payment of rent

Where the lease has been forfeited by peaceable re-entry:

- The High Court may grant relief under the court's inherent equitable jurisdiction; the County Court has the same power under statute.

- All arrears, interest and costs must be paid for relief to be granted.

- Relief granted to a tenant does not require the grant of a new lease; it continues to hold the premises on all the former terms.

- In the County Court, application must be made within six months of the peaceable re-entry. There is no time limit in the High Court, though an application must be made with reas-onable promptitude, and the six-month time limit in the County Court will be taken as a guide.

- Sub-tenants and mortgagees may apply for relief under s.146(4), Law of Property Act 1925, and should apply as soon as possible after the re-entry, since undue delay may debar relief. As in the case of an application by a tenant, all arrears, interest and costs must be paid for relief to be granted.

- Relief granted to a sub-tenant or mortgagee will take the form of an order for a new lease. The terms of the new lease will reflect those of the forfeited head-lease, rather than those of the former sub-lease. Sub-tenants of part may obtain relief in the form of a new lease of their part of the property, not the entire property, and may be required to pay only a proportionate part of the head-lease arrears.

Where the forfeiture was effected by court proceedings:

- Different statutory provisions apply as between High Court and County Court, though the position in each is similar: relief is granted automatically if all arrears, interest and costs are paid into court before trial. Otherwise, the tenant must apply for relief within six months of enforcement of the order for possession and will be required to pay all arrears, interest and costs, in order to obtain relief. In either case, no new lease is necessary.

- The same provisions apply in relation to relief applications by sub-tenants and mortgages, though again the form that relief takes will generally be the grant of a new lease.

CHAPTER NINE
RELIEF FROM FORFEITURE –
NON-RENT BREACHES

This chapter deals with the availability of relief from forfeiture in relation to non-rent breaches, under s.146(2) and s.146(4), Law of Property Act 1925. It covers the time limits for making an application, and the factors governing the exercise of discretion, including the distinction made between remediable and irremediable breaches, whether a breach is wilful or not, and the reluctance of the courts to give the landlord a disproportionate 'windfall' by refusing relief.

Background to jurisdiction

The opening paragraphs of the previous chapter introduced the topic of relief generally, and it may be useful to refer to them as background to this chapter as well. In that chapter, we considered the various routes to relief from forfeiture for arrears of rent. Relief from forfeiture for other breaches of covenant is attended with much less in the way of procedural complexity, although the factors governing the exercise of the discretion whether to grant relief present some difficult points.

Originally the courts did not recognise a jurisdiction to relieve against forfeiture unless the landlord could be placed in the same position as if the breach had not occurred. This is problematic as regards non-rent breaches, though relief might be granted in cases where the breach had been occasioned by fraud, accident, mistake or surprise (*per* Parker J in *Matthew v Smallwood [1910] 1 Ch 777*).

That jurisdiction survives, despite subsequent statutory intervention, according to the Court of Appeal decision (not appealed on this point) in *Billson v Residential Apartments Ltd [1991] 3 WLR 264*, although the point is not beyond dispute. It is of limited practical significance, though, since a wide jurisdiction to relieve against forfeiture in other cases was conferred by the *Conveyancing and Law of Property Act 1881*, the relevant provisions of which are now reproduced in *s.146, Law of Property Act 1925*.

The application

Tenants

Under *s.146(2), Law of Property Act 1925*, the court has a very wide discretion to relieve a tenant from forfeiture, so restoring the lease, where the landlord is "*proceeding*" to forfeit the lease.

It was held in *Pakwood Transport Ltd v 15 Beauchamp Place Ltd (1977) 36 P & CR 112* that the landlord is "*proceeding*" to forfeit once it has served a s.146 notice, and accordingly an application for relief can be made at that stage. It is not necessary to wait until the landlord has actually forfeited. A pre-emptive application may be made where the landlord is thought to be likely to forfeit by peaceable re-entry, as the pending relief application will support an injunction to prevent that, if necessary (see Chapter 5).

Application cannot be made after the landlord has enforced its order for possession, since the landlord is no longer "*proceeding*" to forfeit. It has 'proceeded', and the forfeiture is complete: *Rogers v Rice [1892] 2 Ch 170*.

Between the first-instance and House of Lords decisions in *Billson v Residential Apartments Ltd [1992] 1 All ER 141*, it briefly appeared that if the landlord had forfeited by peaceable re-entry for a non-rent breach, that brought to an end the period during which application could be made under *s.146(2)*. Applying the same approach as in *Rogers v Rice*, peaceable re-entry completed the forfeiture, and the landlord could no longer be said to be "*proceeding*" to forfeit.

The implications of that were extremely serious. In the event of an irremediable breach (as in *Billson*), the landlord might serve its s.146 notice on the tenant and then forfeit by peaceable re-entry after a short period (13 days in *Billson*). If the tenant did not act quickly, applying for relief before the peaceable re-entry, no application would be possible at all, and the lease would be lost.

The House of Lords took a different view, Lord Templeman explaining it thus:

> "*The right conferred by section 146(2) on a tenant to apply for relief against forfeiture may, without violence to the language, be construed as a right to apply "where a lessor <u>proceeds</u>, by action or otherwise," to enforce a right of re-entry. So construed, section 146(2) enables the tenant to apply for relief whenever and however the landlord claims that the lease has been determined for breach of covenant.*"

Application can therefore be made after a peaceable re-entry, but:

> "*the court in deciding whether to grant relief will take into account all the circumstances including delay on the part of the tenant*".

The contrast with rent-breach cases is striking. There, a relief application can be made up to six months after the landlord has enforced an order for possession, and perhaps more than six months after a peaceable re-entry, if applying in the High Court. In non-rent cases, execution of an order for possession closes off the possibility of applying for relief completely, and undue delay in applying after a peaceable re-entry may also bar relief.

Derivative interest-holders

Where sub-tenants and mortgagees are concerned, relief is available under *s.146(4)*, as it is in the case of a rent breach, where the landlord has peaceably re-entered. However, this jurisdiction does not extend to equitable chargees: *Bland v Ingram's Estates Ltd [2001] 2 EGLR 23*.

The outcome of a successful application will be an order for the grant of a new lease to the applicant (*Cadogan v Dimovic [1984] 2 All ER 168*). In the case of an application by a mortgagee, the new lease would be held subject to the mortgagor's equity of redemption. The basis on which the terms of such a new lease might be determined was covered in the previous chapter, where *s.146(4)* is considered at greater length.

It was held in *Escalus Properties Ltd v Robinson [1995] 4 All ER 852* that the definition of 'lessee' in relation to *s.146(2)* is wide enough to include a mortgagee by sub-demise, so such a party has a choice between applying under *s.146(2)* and *s.146(4)*. Which is preferable may be largely influenced by the difference in the form of relief: reinstatement of the former lease, or grant of a new lease.

The rules as to when application can be made under *s.146(4)* are the same as they are, post-*Billson*, in relation to applications under *s.146(2)*: *Rexhaven v Nurse [1995] EGCS 125*. Thus, application may be made after a peaceable re-entry: a matter of particular importance to sub-tenants and mortgagees, who might well not have been served with a copy of the s.146 notice.

Exercise of discretion

The court is required under *s.146(2)* to have regard to:

> "*the proceedings and conduct of the parties under the foregoing provisions of this section, and to all the other circumstances*".

Relief may be granted on:

> "*such terms, if any, as to costs, expenses, damages, compensation, penalty, or otherwise, including the granting of an injunction to restrain any like breach in the future, as the court, in the circumstances of each case, thinks fit*".

Evidently the discretion is very wide, as the cases illustrate.

The same is true under *s.146(4)*, although the two sub-sections are worded differently, and the following consideration of the factors which have been found to be relevant in the exercise of the discretion does not distinguish between the two provisions. However, it is worth mentioning that in the case of *s.146(4)* the courts have on occasion observed that the discretion should be exercised sparingly, because it may involve placing the landlord into a direct relationship with a tenant whom he has never approved (*Creery v Summersell* and *Flowerdew & Co Ltd 1949 1 Ch 751*). This is particularly relevant where the breach consists of a sub-letting without the landlord's consent (*Imray v Oakshette [1897] 2 QB 218*; *Matthews v Smallwood [1910] 1 Ch 777*).

Irremediable breaches

As a general principle, all breaches of covenant must be remedied in order to obtain relief: *Hyman v Rose [1912] AC 623*. That should logically mean that relief will be unavailable in the case of a breach which the law regards as irremediable; unfortunately, the distinction between remediable and irremediable breaches is highly unsatisfactory and confused.

Immoral or illegal user

Breach of a covenant against immoral or illegal user is often said to be irremediable, because of the stigma which attaches to the premises as a result. The notion of stigma was explained by Maugham LJ in the Court of Appeal in *Governors of Rugby School v Tannahill [1935] 1 KB 87*, as follows:

> "*The use of the premises for a long period for an immoral purpose ser-iously tends to damage their value and to give them a bad name, as indeed is shown by the common designation of such premises – namely, a house of ill-fame; and merely ceasing for a reasonable time, perhaps a few weeks or a month, to use the premises for an immoral purpose would be no remedy for the breach of covenant which had been committed over a long period.*"

However, it is clear that such a breach will not be considered irre-mediable in all circumstances. In *Vanezis v Ozkoc [2018] All ER (D) 52 (Jul)*, a case concerning alleged use of the premises for the purpose of a criminal conspiracy to sell Class A drugs, the judge observed:

"There is no rule of law that the exercise of discretion allowing relief from forfeiture must always be refused in such cases. That would be to deny the discretionary jurisdiction conferred on the court by statute."

As the passage quoted from the *Tannahill* case suggests, whether the breach of covenant has caused any stigma to attach to the premises is a judgment to be made in each case. The length of time for which the breach has persisted may be relevant. The breach will be found to be irremediable if it is considered that any stigma will persist for a lengthy period, even though the immoral user itself might be discontinued quite promptly. As was remarked by Slade LJ in *Expert Clothing Service & Sales Ltd v Hillgate House Ltd [1986] Ch 340*:

"…mere cesser by the tenant of the offending use within a reasonable period … could not have remedied the breaches because it could not have removed the stigma which they had caused to attach to the premises."

It may also be relevant, where the breach is committed by a sub-tenant, whether the head-tenant knew of the breach, and what was the nature of their response when informed of it. In *Glass v Kencakes Ltd [1966] 1 QB 611*, the use of the premises for prostitution was unknown to the head-tenant before service of the s.146 notice, and the prostitutes were evicted as soon as possible thereafter. There was no evidence that the premises had acquired a bad reputation, or that the value was affected. The breach was held to be capable of remedy within a reasonable time. A similar set of circumstances led to the same conclusion in *Patel v K&J Restaurants [2010] EWCA Civ 1211*; a conclusion supported by the trial judge's striking finding that, given the nature of the surrounding area, no stigma would have attached to the property. (Tottenham Court Road in central London, for the curious).

Negative and positive covenants

There was a suggestion in the first instance judgment in *Governors of Rugby School v Tannahill [1934] 1 KB 695* that the reason the immoral user was to be considered irremediable was because it was a breach of a negative covenant:

> "*A promise to do a thing, if broken, can be remedied by the thing being done. But breach of a promise not to do a thing cannot in any true sense be remedied; that which was done cannot be undone.*"

As the expression goes, you can't unring a bell. While true, that is a not a helpful starting-point for making a value judgment about whether a tenant should be relieved of the consequences of their actions. The approach was rejected by the Court of Appeal in that case, but subsequently picked up and taken further in *Scala House & District Property v Forbes [1974] QB 575*, another Court of Appeal authority. There, a breach of a covenant not to assign or sub-let was held to be irremediable, and the 'stigma' cases were explained on the ground that breach of a negative covenant could never be capable of remedy.

The principles were much discussed in *Expert Clothing Service and Sales Ltd v Hillgate House Ltd [1985] 2 EGLR 85*, where the Court of Appeal confined the *Scala* decision to once-and-for-all breaches of a negative covenant. The approach taken there was that whether a breach was remediable depended on whether the harm caused to the landlord could be put right, in practical terms. A distinction was suggested between cases involving stigma, and others. As O'Connor LJ remarked:

> "*To stop doing what is forbidden by a negative covenant may or may not remedy the breach… Thus to remove the window boxes and pay for the repair of any damage done will remedy the breach but to stop using the house as a brothel will not, because the taint lingers on…*"

In *Billson v Residential Apartments Ltd [1991] 3 All ER 265*, for example, it was doubted whether the first instance judge had correctly characterised the carrying out of alterations without landlord's consent as an irremediable breach. In *Savva v Hussein (1996) 73 P & CR 150* breaches of negative covenants, not to change the exterior sign and not to alter the premises without consent, were held to be remediable. Stoughton LJ said:

> "*When something has been done without consent … it is a remedy if the mischief caused by the breach can be removed. In the case of a covenant not to make alterations without consent or not to display signs without consent, if there is a breach of that, the mischief can be removed by removing the signs or restoring the property to the state it was in before the alterations.*"

Scala House was criticised in characteristically trenchant terms by Neuberger LJ in *Akici v LR Butlin Ltd [2006] 1 W.L.R. 201:*

> "*the reasoning of the leading judgment in the case is, at least in part, demonstrably fallacious and inconsistent with common sense and many other authorities; … it has been overtaken and marginalised by the Expert Clothing and Savva cases.*"

Nevertheless, he felt compelled by precedent to accept that it stands as authority for the proposition that breach of a covenant against assignment or subletting without landlord's consent is irremediable.

In summary, it seems to be a general rule of thumb that breach of a positive covenant (repairing covenants, most obviously) will be capable of remedy, since a failure to do something can always be remedied by doing it. It does not follow that breach of a negative covenant must be irremediable, though breach of a covenant against assignment or subletting always is. Other once-and-for-all breaches of negative covenants may be remediable, and there is no reason why a continuing breach of a negative covenant should be regarded as irremediable. The presence or absence of stigma may be a deciding factor in the case of negative covenants.

While that summary presents a confused picture, what is undeniable is that the categories of breach regarded as being irremediable have narrowed. There is a useful discussion of the caselaw and the modern understanding in In *Vanezis v Ozkoc [2018] All ER (D) 52 (Jul).* The case was decided in the Mayor's and City of London Court, and hence is not a binding precedent, but the judgment of Steven Gee QC is a long and careful one, which examines authorities on waiver and relief from forfeiture thoroughly, and has a number of useful observations:

"In my judgment, [the authorities] approve an approach under section 146 on the issue of whether a breach is capable of remedy, of looking to the future, and considering whether the mischief done by the breach can be remedied looking at the matter practically and without technicalities. Most types of breaches should in principle be capable of remedy, subject to the particular facts and circumstances of the case..."

"Whether relief from forfeiture is to be granted on the particular facts, is a question of discretion. There is no rule of law that the exercise of discretion allowing relief from forfeiture must always be refused in such cases [illegal use of premises, including illegal use in connection with very serious criminal conduct]. *That would be to deny the discretionary jurisdiction conferred on the court by statute. This includes, in my judgment, consideration of whether forfeiture of the lease would confer on the landlords a benefit out of proportion to the loss which they had suffered by reason of the breach".*

Wilful breaches

It is a general principle of equity's jurisdiction to relieve against the consequences of a breach that it should not be 'wilful', in the sense that the tenant deliberately breaches an obligation, in full knowledge of it: *Shiloh Spinners v Harding [1973] AC 691*. It was held in that case that relief from the consequences of a wilful breach should only be granted in exceptional cases.

The view was taken in *Southern Depot Co Ltd v British Railways Board [1990] 2 EGLR 39* that the principle applied only to the court's inherent jurisdiction to grant relief, and not to the jurisdiction under *s.146(2)*, though it would be a relevant factor in such cases too. In that case the judge considered that it did not need to be an exceptional case to justify granting relief under *s.146(2)* in relation to a wilful breach, and relief was granted accordingly. However, the enquiry as to whether the breach was wilful is one which features regularly in forfeiture cases.

In the context of alienation, it may occur that a tenant assigns or sub-lets without obtaining landlord's consent, in breach of covenant. In *Eastern Telegraph Co v Dent [1899] 1 QB 835*, the tenant sub-let part of the premises to a party already in occupation, without landlord's consent, and it was found that no reasonable objection could have been raised by the landlord. However, there had been no request for consent, and that omission made the breach a 'wilful' one, debarring the tenant from relief. It was considered that it would not justify a grant of relief that the failure to seek consent might have been through forgetfulness, or because the tenant thought it unimportant.

That case was not in argument before the Privy Council in *Lam Kee Ying v Lam Shes Tong [1975] AC 247*, another case where there had been no application for consent. Here, though, relief was considered to be appropriate on the basis that there could have been no reasonable objection if consent had been sought. That case was very different from *Eastern Telegraph*, though, involving a family business deciding to incorporate, and thereby parting with possession to the new company.

It would be rash for a tenant to conclude that the formality of asking for consent can safely be dispensed with where the landlord could not reasonably withhold consent if applied for.

On the other hand, if consent has been sought, but unreasonably refused by the landlord, despite the presence in the alienation clause of a proviso that landlord's consent should not be unreasonably withheld, the tenant can proceed with the transaction lawfully: *Treloar v Bigge (1874) LR 9 Ex 151*, and (in the context of consent to alterations) *Old Grovebury Manor Farm Ltd v Seymour Plant Sales and Hire Ltd (No. 2) [1979] 1 WLR 1397*. In such a case there is no breach of covenant, so that there is no right to forfeit, and no need for a grant of relief.

An example of the continued relevance of the enquiry whether the breach was 'wilful' is provided by *Patel v K&J Restaurants [2010]*

EWCA Civ 1211. There, the leased property comprised restaurant premises on the ground floor and basement, and flats on the first, second and third floors, which were sub-let. There were two breaches of covenant:

- one of the flats was being used by the sub-tenant for prostitution; and

- the tenant had appointed another company, MPC, to manage the restaurant. On the facts, this amounted to having parted with possession.

In relation to the immoral user, the court held it was not a wilful breach because the tenant was unaware of it, and took immediate steps to recover possession of the flat once notified of it. As regards the restaurant, this breach was not wilful either; the tenant had believed that it was simply appointing a manager, and had had no thought of parting with possession. (In this respect, the facts are notably akin to those of the *Lam Kee Ying* case). Moreover, it was attempting to exclude MPC from the premises. The court was therefore able to order relief on terms.

Windfall to landlord

Another factor which is commonly found in the caselaw is the courts' reluctance to give the landlord a 'windfall' out of all proportion to the damage suffered by the landlord, by bringing to an end a lease with a significant capital value, or by giving the landlord possession significantly ahead of time. This factor was present in the *Patel* case, where it was found that possession would give the landlord a very substantial windfall, enabling it to recover possession 14 years early; while assuming terms of relief could be complied with, no lasting damage would have been suffered.

In *Ul-Hassan v Magnic Ltd [2015] EWCA Civ 224* the defendants' son had acquired by assignment a rack-rented sub-lease of a property for 16 years from 2002. His parents, the defendants, had subsequently acquired the head-lease, which was for a term of 125 years from 1980, at a ground rent, and had a capital value of £150,000. The son began to operate a pizza takeaway business on the premises without planning permission, which was a breach of covenant under both the head-lease and the sub-lease.

Forfeiture proceedings were issued, and compromised on the basis that the son would regularise the planning position. However, when planning permission was applied for, there were problems over installing a suitable ventilation system. The matter returned to court on a number of occasions over a lengthy period, to vary the terms of relief so as to allow further time for dealing with the planning authority. One point which emerges from the decision of the Court of Appeal is that protracted non-compliance with conditions which have been imposed to secure relief from forfeiture is not necessarily sufficient to determine that further relief should not be granted.

The son had continued to trade beyond a longstop date specified in the terms of relief despite the continued absence of planning permission. However, he had genuinely (and on legal advice) believed that a compromise agreement had entitled him to do so. When a previous hearing had confirmed that he was not entitled to continue trading, he had promptly ceased to do so, and in all the circumstances his breach had not been wilful. His continued trading had not harmed the claimants in any way.

The District Judge had had regard to the windfall that forfeiture would give to the claimants, given the capital value of the head-lease, but had nevertheless refused further relief. The Court of Appeal reversed that decision, implying that the windfall argument was of greater significance where a breach was not wilful.

Terms of relief

If relief is granted, the usual costs order is for the tenant to pay the landlord's costs on an indemnity basis, even though it is the tenant who has succeeded in its application for relief. This is because the forfeiture has been prompted by the tenant's default. The rule was doubted by

Lord Templeman in *Billson v Residential Apartments Ltd [1992] 1 All ER 141*, but it has since been confirmed in the Court of Appeal in *Patel v K&J Restaurants [2010] EWCA Civ 1211*.

Otherwise the terms will be directed at remedying, in a practical sense, the damage caused by the breaches of covenant. A good recent illustration of the breadth of the court's discretion is *Freifeld v West Kensington Court Ltd [2015] EWCA Civ 806*, in which the landlord sought to forfeit a head-lease for a breach of the alienation covenant. The tenant had granted a sub-lease of what was described as a "*controversially run Chinese restaurant*". There was a background of unsatisfactory conduct by the tenant, both in failing to 'police' the restaurant user and in relation to insurance.

There was significant value in the head-lease, and the issue was whether the windfall the landlord would gain from forfeiture should mean that the tenant should nevertheless obtain relief. The Court of Appeal held that it should, but only following surrender of the sub-lease and on terms that the tenant would both (a) appoint competent managing agents and (b) find a suitable assignee of the head-lease. There was a further condition imposed that forfeiture should automatically take effect if no contract for assignment were exchanged within 6 months.

Thus, the landlord would get rid of the tenant, but the tenant would be able to realise the value in its lease, although not on a timescale of its own choosing.

Insolvency of tenant

Insolvency of the tenant will be considered an irremediable breach: *Civil Service Co-operative Society Ltd v McGrigor's Trustee [1923] 2 Ch 347; Fryer v Ewart [1902] AC 187*. Nevertheless, relief may still be granted, typically in order to allow the insolvency practitioner to market the lease. A recent example was *SHB Realisations Ltd v Cribbs Mall Nominees [2019] Lexis Citation 32*, which brings together a number of the factors we have considered.

In 1998, BHS took a 125-year lease of a unit at Cribbs Causeway shopping centre in Bristol at a peppercorn rent, but paying a premium of £7.05m plus VAT. The lease included a keep-open covenant, which required BHS to open its shop seven days a week during specified opening hours.

Following the administration of BHS, the store closed permanently on 28 August 2016 rendering BHS (now SHB Realisations) in breach of its keep-open covenant. As a result, the landlord sought to forfeit. Not only was the insolvency an irremediable breach, but in practice so was the breach of keep-open covenant, since there was no prospect of the tenant resuming trading.

SHB applied for relief from forfeiture for a period of six months, to allow further time to assign the lease. It argued that attempts to market the lease to date (over a period of 36 months) had been hindered by the ongoing litigation.

The court had regard to the following factors:

- SHB was in deliberate breach of covenant, not caused by third parties, though it could not be said to be wilful.

- The breach of covenant could not be remedied until an assignee could be found who would trade from the store. In the meantime, the landlord was suffering ongoing damage, as were their other tenants, by virtue of the impact of the closure upon the shopping centre generally.

- The lease was an asset which was once of considerable value, and still had a value of over £1m. There was a real market for the lease, and a real rather than fanciful prospect of finding an assignee, and SHB should not be deprived of the opportunity to reduce its debts.

Balancing the position of both parties, it was held that there should be relief from forfeiture, conditional on an assignment of the lease being completed within a period of just under three months.

Summary

Where forfeiture relies upon a non-rent breach of covenant, relief is available to tenants under s.146(2), and to sub-tenants and mortgagees under s.146(4), Law of Property Act 1925.

Application may be made before forfeiture, once a s.146 notice has been served. It may not be made after enforcement of an order for possession. It may be made after a peaceable re-entry, but undue delay may count against the applicant.

The discretion is a wide one. Certain factors recur in the caselaw:

- Generally, breaches of covenant must be remedied in order to obtain relief. Although there is confusion in the caselaw as to what breaches are not capable of remedy, the courts are increasingly reluctant to find that a breach is irremediable, and will usually apply a test of whether the damage suffered by the landlord can be put right in a practical sense.

- Breach of a covenant against immoral use may well be thought irremediable, if the court concludes that a stigma will attach to the premises as a result.

- The courts will not usually relieve against the consequences of a 'wilful' breach of covenant.

- Relief may be granted to prevent the landlord receiving a disproportionate windfall from the recovery of possession.

- Insolvency of the tenant does not prevent the grant of relief, where there is a prospect of the tenant finding a suitable assignee for the lease.

CHAPTER TEN
DOCUMENTING SETTLEMENTS
AND RE-LETTING

This chapter addresses some practicalities arising after forfeiture: how any settlement with the tenant should be documented, and how to tackle the risk of an application for relief being made after the property has been re-let.

Documenting settlements

Resisting informal settlements

The forfeiture process may lead to the final recovery of possession; alternatively it may lead to a settlement whereby all breaches of covenant are addressed to the landlord's satisfaction. That may have been the landlord's aim in the first place, but if the objective was instead to regain possession, remedy of the breaches makes it unrealistic for the landlord to expect to achieve that. The only remaining issue will be how to document the settlement, or indeed whether it is necessary to do so at all, if all necessary remedial action has been completed.

Settlement discussions with the tenant will, it may be assumed, have taken place after forfeiture. Up until then, the landlord will have adopted the standard precautions against waiver, and suspended all contact. The tenant is apt to have thought this unreasonable of the landlord, even aggressive, when (from its point of view) the matter might have been sorted out quickly and easily in a without prejudice conversation.

Once settlement terms have been agreed with the tenant, they may expect that the situation can immediately be normalised, without any formality or further expenditure on legal fees. Particularly since they will have had to accept liability for the landlord's costs of the forfeiture as well as their own, further legal spend will be unwelcome. Neither will the tenant see any reason for delay, especially if the lease was forfeited by peaceable re-entry, so that they are out of possession, and pressing for re-admission to the property.

It will therefore raise the temperature even more for the landlord to insist upon further legal formalities before normal relations can resume, however in most cases the landlord must resist an informal settlement. It is sometimes necessary to be very firm on this. A tenant who is out of occupation may perhaps be given access pending satisfactory document-ation of the settlement, but only on terms which safeguard the landlord's right to possession, such as a tenancy at will.

The reason for this is that forfeiture is generally irrevocable, as previ-ously discussed. While the forfeited lease may be revived by a grant of relief, it cannot be revived by simply proceeding as if the lease were reinstated, which would almost certainly give rise to an implied periodic tenancy instead. Security of tenure would attach to it under the *Landlord and Tenant Act 1954*, there would be uncertainty as to its terms, and ascertaining the appropriate length of notice required to ter-minate it might be problematic.

Putting a tenant back into possession while avoiding that result therefore requires a degree of formality, usually in the form of a grant of relief from forfeiture. That will mean the tenant must incur some addi-tional legal expenditure. It is only possible for the court to grant relief if it has been applied for, so if that has not been done, it will be necessary to do it now. Then the terms of relief will need to be drafted.

There is an alternative solution, which is that a new lease might be granted to the tenant. That will also require legal input, of course, and moreover the tenant will have to pay Stamp Duty Land Tax on it (subject to any available reliefs). Drafting of a new lease could poten-tially be simplified by incorporating the terms of the forfeited lease by reference.

In the usual case, though, whichever option the parties take, the further delay and expense need not actually be that great. How matters can best be documented depends upon the method of forfeiture adopted, the nature of the breach, who is the relief applicant, and the tenant's response to the forfeiture up to that point. It will assist in considering the various possibilities to have in mind the rules governing the grant of relief, set out in Chapters 8 and 9.

Terms of settlement

Remedying of the breach of covenant complained of is of course central to relief from forfeiture. If the breach is purely monetary, it can usually be expected that all sums due will have been paid prior to the landlord signing any consent order or other settlement document, in which case there is no need to include any terms for payment.

It may be, however, that the landlord will have been persuaded to agree further time to pay, perhaps by way of instalments, and perhaps it will in turn have required the provision of some additional security for payment in future. Those matters would need to be provided for in the settlement terms.

As regards other breaches, what the landlord will be prepared to accept as sufficient remedy will be fact-dependent, and will require express provision.

- Breach of use restrictions may obviously be remedied by discontinuance of the offending use, and again it is likely that that will already have been done prior to documenting the settlement. The landlord may perhaps be prepared to accept a change in use upon certain conditions (e.g. change from retail sale of antiquarian books to that of drum kits, conditional upon specified sound-proofing measures).

- Breach of covenant against alterations can be remedied by reinstatement of the premises, but the landlord may alternatively be prepared to accept the works done, with some modifications, or payment of financial compensation.

- The appropriate remedy for breach of repairing covenant is obviously going to be carrying out repairs, though usually some time-limit will be agreed, and perhaps the landlord will accept that some works may be deferred, or can be omitted altogether.

The negotiating parameters will of course be what each party considers to be the terms of relief that the court would impose, in the absence of agreement.

There may well be issues as to financial liabilities in relation to the period between forfeiture and relief, particularly where a tenant or sub-tenant has broken back in and re-occupied following a peaceable re-entry. Payment of mesne profits will need to be dealt with, and perhaps apportioned between head-tenant and sub-tenant of part; other outgoings may include business rates and insurance, for example.

If the settlement is with a sub-tenant or mortgagee, in relation to an application under *s.146(4)*, *Law of Property Act 1925*, so that relief will take the form of the grant of a new lease, then clearly the terms of the new lease must be provided for. The terms which the court might order are considered in Chapter 8, and of course particular difficulties may arise if it is to be a new lease of part. It will often be best to annexe the form of new lease to the settlement documentation.

Parties to settlement

Where it is the tenant that applies for relief, under whichever jurisdiction, the lease will be restored by the grant of relief (*s.38(2)*, *Senior Courts Act 1981*), and a consent order granting relief to the tenant will therefore restore all derivative interests as well, so that sub-tenants and mortgagees often need not be parties.

On the other hand, it may be a default by a sub-tenant which led to the forfeiture in the first place. If, say, a sub-tenant carried out alterations to the property in breach of covenant, the head-tenant will need the sub-tenant (assuming it is willing and able to take the required action to remedy the breach) to be party to the settlement, so that it can take on responsibility for the necessary remedial action, plus the landlord's and head-tenant's costs, plus any financial liabilities arising between forfeiture and relief.

In a case where a derivative interest-holder is the relief applicant, under *s.146(4)*, a grant of relief in the form of a new lease direct to the applicant will not affect the tenant, and hence they need not be a party to the proceedings or to the settlement: *Abbey National Building Society v Maybeech Ltd [1985] 1 Ch 190*. The applicant may be looking to recover costs from the tenant, though, and if that has been agreed then the tenant needs to be a party.

Settlement after peaceable re-entry

If an application for relief has already been made, so much the better, but that will not necessarily be the case:

- If the landlord effected forfeiture based upon arrears of rent, and if the applicant is the tenant, jurisdiction to grant relief is under the High Court's inherent equitable jurisdiction, or in the County Court under *s.139(2), County Courts Act 1984*. The tenant will have had up to six months after peaceable re-entry to make the application, and may not yet have done so.

- If the forfeiture was based upon a non-rent breach, and the tenant's claim to relief arises under *s.146(2), Law of Property Act 1925*, it should have applied promptly after peaceable re-entry to avoid the risk of losing the right to relief through undue delay.

- The same applies to a sub-tenant or mortgagee, where the claim to relief after peaceable re-entry is under *s.146(4), Law of Property Act 1925*, in relation to both rent and non-rent breaches.

Once relief has been applied for, it is possible to document the settlement by means of a consent order. Thought must be given to whether any party other than the applicant needs to be party to the proceedings in order to be bound by the settlement (see above), and if so they must be joined.

In the case of a settlement arrived at with a sub-tenant or mortgagee, since the grant of relief must result in a new lease in any case, the parties may find it simpler just to execute the lease without going to the trouble of a consent order, particularly if there has been no application for relief as yet. The landlord would presumably collect payment of its costs and any other settlement sums upon completion.

It would be open to the parties to proceed in that way where the applicant for relief is the tenant, too, although as mentioned that would potentially involve Stamp Duty Land Tax liability.

Form of consent order

The basic structure of a consent order for relief will be straightforward, though complicated terms of settlement may obviously require detailed drafting. It will either be made in the course of the landlord's forfeiture proceedings, or in the course of the applicant's stand-alone relief proceedings, following peaceable re-entry.

- If the order is being made in the landlord's forfeiture proceedings, it will begin with an order for possession in the landlord's favour. If made in the applicant's relief proceedings, the order may instead usefully begin by reciting the fact of the peaceable re-entry.

- If the breaches of covenant have already been remedied, it will recite that.

- There will then follow an order that relief be granted, setting out any terms of relief.

- If the applicant is a sub-tenant or mortgagee, the order will need to detail the terms of the new lease which is to be granted to them. It may be easiest to attach an agreed form of lease to the order. A deadline for completion may be expected to be included, and perhaps also requirements for the tenant to comply with all necessary registration formalities.

- If the order is made in the landlord's forfeiture proceedings, it will deal as appropriate with the other relief claimed by the landlord, e.g. mesne profits and interest. If the order is made in the applicant's relief proceedings, it will need to deal with any other relief claimed by the applicant, e.g. a claim for a declaration that the forfeiture was unlawful might be dismissed.

- If any of the settlement terms are still to be performed, relief will be conditional upon performance, so that the order will state that the landlord is to be given possession in default.

- The order will conclude by dealing with costs; usually the tenant will pay the landlord's costs, to be assessed on an indemnity basis.

Settlement after forfeiture by court proceedings

Arrears of rent

In the event of forfeiture by court proceedings, based upon arrears of rent, automatic relief is available upon payment of arrears, interest and costs before trial, in accordance with *ss.210-212, Common Law Procedure Act 1852* (High Court), and *s.138, County Courts Act 1984* (County Court). These provisions apply to tenants, sub-tenants and mortgagees alike. The lease is restored, with all derivative interests, and no documentation of the settlement or grant of relief is required, beyond a stay of the proceedings.

Under either of those statutory schemes, if payment is made, not before trial, but within six months of the landlord enforcing an order for possession, then relief must be applied for, and a simple consent order restoring the lease will be appropriate.

As detailed in Chapter 8:

- if the arrears amounted to less than six months' rent, an application by the tenant for relief in the High Court would be under the court's inherent equitable jurisdiction;

- in either High Court or County Court, application by sub-tenants or mortgagees for relief in rent-breach cases might equally be made under *s.146(4), Law of Property Act 1925*, as well as under the 1852 or 1984 Acts.

Either eventuality would require documentation of the settlement by the grant of relief in a consent order, as in the case of settlement after peaceable re-entry. Again, the parties could opt for the grant of a new lease instead

Other breaches

The position is rather simpler in non-rent cases. Relief may be granted to tenants under *s.146(2)* of the 1925 Act, and to sub-tenants or mortgagees under *s.146(4)*. Again, if there has as yet been no application for relief, then one must be made, if a grant of relief is to be documented. In defended proceedings, though, the landlord's right to forfeit will usually be disputed, and relief will have been sought by way of counter-claim.

As above, an obvious way forward is to agree a consent order, while proceeding to a new lease instead is an alternative.

There may be other options in these cases, though. If the proceedings have been defended, then on the strength of *Mount Cook Land Ltd v The Media Business Centre Ltd [2004] EWHC 348 (Ch)* and *Hynes v Twinsectra [1995] 71 P&CR 145* (see Chapter 6) the lease may be restored satisfactorily either by the landlord discontinuing the proceedings, or by a dismissal of the landlord's claim by consent. Either option would of course require other settlement terms to have been already performed, or recorded effectively in a separate agreement.

If the proceedings have not been defended, then it seems that those options are unavailable. In any event, the parties might still prefer to have the reassurance of a consent order or new lease, rather than relying on some slightly elusive caselaw.

Re-letting

If the landlord has forfeited a lease, and then re-let the property to a third party, there is potentially a problem if an application for relief is made subsequently. A grant of relief which resulted in the third party being evicted from the premises would on the face of it give rise to a claim against the landlord for breach of quiet enjoyment, or derogation from grant.

That consideration could inhibit the landlord from re-letting; moreover, it might not always be clear how long the landlord would have to wait before there was no longer a risk of a relief application. In the event of a peaceable re-entry for non-payment of rent, where relief is available to the tenant in the High Court under its inherent equitable jurisdiction, there is no time limit. While it would usually be expected that no application would be permitted beyond six months after the peaceable re-entry, an application made as much as 14 months after-wards was allowed in *Pineport Ltd v Grangeglen Ltd [2016] EWHC 1318 (Ch)*.

Even where there is certainty as to the risk period, it may be lengthy. A landlord who forfeits for arrears of rent, by means of court proceedings, cannot rely on there being no possibility of a relief application until six months after enforcement of the order for possession.

If the tenant has led the landlord to believe that there would be no application for relief, then the landlord may feel relatively safe in pro-ceeding to complete a new letting, since that factor might well lead to a refusal of relief: *Silverman v AFCO [1988] 1 EGLR 51*. Equally, the potential applicant's equity to seek relief against forfeiture should not affect the incoming third-party tenant if they did not have notice of it: *Fuller v Judy Properties Ltd [1992] 14 EG 106.*

The latter case demonstrates a possible means of resolving such situations: relief was granted on the basis that the restored lease should take effect in reversion to that which had by then been granted to the new tenant. The new tenant was therefore entitled to remain in occupation, but liable to pay rent to the former tenant, which was in turn liable for the rent under the restored lease. The landlord therefore faced no claim for breach of quiet enjoyment, the innocent third party continued to enjoy occupation of the premises, and the successful relief applicant became entitled to a profit rental of £9,000 per annum.

That is simply an example of the exercise of discretion in one case, and does not lay down any principle. The court was assisted in reaching this decision by the fact that the relief applicant could not beneficially occupy the premises itself owing to inability to obtain planning consent for change of use. As ever, individual circumstances must influence the exercise of the discretion.

There is a number of measures which a landlord might take before re-letting, in order to reduce or avoid the risk of a successful application for relief.

- Disclosure to an incoming tenant of the potential for a claim for relief has the considerable drawback that it may discourage them from proceeding with the letting, particularly since the fact that they have notice of the equity to seek relief against forfeiture deprives them of protection against it. However, if they remain prepared to proceed after disclosure, then the risk is transferred to them, and there can be no claim for breach of quiet enjoyment or derogation from grant.

- An option with fewer drawbacks attached is to notify all potential relief applicants of the forthcoming letting, and give them an opportunity (probably at least two weeks from the notification) to apply for relief, before completing the letting.

- The best protection is to obtain from the court a declaration that there should be no grant of relief. Where forfeiture has been effected by court proceedings, the relief claimed in the action may include this declaration. So long as the court is satisfied that the proceedings have been served on all potential applicants for relief, there should be no reason why the declaration could not be granted, if none of them has taken the opportunity to apply.

  If the forfeiture proceeded by way of peaceable re-entry, on the other hand, the landlord would have to issue stand-alone proceedings seeking this declaration. Again, if the court is satisfied that such proceedings have been served on all potential applicants, there is no reason why the declaration could not be made. The practical problem might be the length of time taken to obtain the declaration in such circumstances.

It should be noted that in some situations there will be no risk, or least only a slight one. Where the potential application would be made pursuant to *s.146(2)* or *s.146(4)* of the 1925 Act:

- if the landlord has proceeded by way of court proceedings, and has got as far as execution of an order for possession, then there is no risk, since no application for relief is possible at that stage; and

- if the landlord has proceeded by peaceable re-entry, then undue delay may bar an application for relief, so that the risk should diminish rapidly after forfeiture.

This consideration might perhaps be taken into account in the decision as to which method of forfeiture to adopt.

Summary

Where landlord and tenant reach settlement terms following forfeiture, there may be pressure from the tenant to proceed as if the former lease were reinstated, without any formal steps being taken to achieve that.

The landlord must resist any such informal reinstatement, since the likely result will be an implied periodic tenancy.

Instead the landlord must insist on either a grant of relief from forfeiture in a consent order, or the grant of a new lease. Which is the best option will depend on all the circumstances and the history of the forfeiture to date.

Re-letting after a forfeiture presents complications in that the potential for a grant of relief exposes the landlord to claims for breach of quiet enjoyment or derogation from grant. The risk may be mitigated or removed by disclosing it to an incoming tenant, notifying potential relief applicants of the forthcoming letting, or by obtaining from the court a declaration that no relief should be granted.

CHAPTER ELEVEN
FORFEITURE AND TENANT INSOLVENCY

This chapter covers the restrictions placed upon the ability to forfeit by the various insolvency procedures.

Forfeiture provisions generally entitle the landlord to forfeit the lease in the event of the tenant going into an insolvency procedure, and insolvency will be considered to be irremediable: *Civil Service Co-operative Society Ltd v McGrigor's Trustee [1923] 2 Ch 347*; *Fryer v Ewart [1902] AC 187*. However, the various insolvency procedures impose significant restrictions upon the landlord's remedies, including the right to forfeit, whether by peaceable re-entry or by court proceedings, and whether in the case of individual insolvency or corporate insolvency.

As a general rule, therefore, if opportunity allows, a landlord who believes that its tenant is on the verge of insolvency should be thinking about exercising its available remedies (not just forfeiture) as soon as possible, before insolvency prevents it from doing so.

Moreover, if the landlord overcomes these restrictions and exercises the right to forfeit, there is no guarantee of recovering possession, since relief may be available despite the irremediable nature of the event, typically in order to allow the insolvency practitioner to market the lease. A recent example was *SHB Realisations Ltd v Cribbs Mall Nominees [2019] Lexis Citation 32*, considered in Chapter 9.

Although there may be obstacles in the way of recovering possession from a tenant or insolvency practitioner who does not wish to give it up, it is of course an easy matter to recover possession, despite the insolvency, where they no longer require the premises. Forfeiture may be effected with the consent of an administrator, without the need to obtain the leave of the court, and while the legislation does not provide for other office-holders to consent to forfeiture, nevertheless it is usually straightforward to arrange for a surrender of the lease.

In the event of a compulsory liquidation, consent of the court to a surrender is required under s.*127, Insolvency Act 1986,* (see *OfficeServe Technologies Ltd v Anthony-Mike [2017] EWHC 1920 (Ch)*), though the liquidator will obtain this easily enough. The same requirement applies in bankruptcy, under *s.284.* Also, a liquidator has power to disclaim the lease (assuming that it can be regarded as 'onerous property', as it usually can) under *s.178,* and can be prompted to do so by service of a notice to elect whether to disclaim under *s.178(6).* The equivalent provision in bankruptcy is in *ss.315-316.* At least in cases where there is no sub-tenant or mortgagee who might complicate matters by applying for a vesting order, disclaimer represents a quick and cheap route to lease termination.

Insolvency of individual tenant

<u>Bankruptcy</u>

The *Insolvency Act 1986, s.285* (reproducing predecessor provisions in earlier legislation) restricts the exercise of remedies when a bankruptcy petition is pending, or an individual has been made bankrupt. In such circumstances, any action, execution or other legal process against the property or person of the debtor in respect of the debt may be stayed under *s.285(1)* and *(2).* Further, under *s.285(3),* after the making of a bankruptcy order no creditor shall have any remedy against the property or person of the bankrupt in respect of the debt, or commence any action or other legal proceedings against the bankrupt in respect of the debt, except with the leave of the court.

While this sounds like a comprehensive moratorium, it was held in *Ezekiel v Orakpo [1976] 3 All ER 659* that forfeiture of a lease for non-payment of rent was not a "*remedy against the property ... of the debtor in respect of the debt*", but was the determination of the lessee's right to remain in possession of the property because of its breach of a covenant under the lease. Therefore, leave was not required to issue forfeiture proceedings under *s.285(3)*, and such proceedings should not be stayed under *s.285(1)* or *(2)*.

This was followed in *Razzaq v Pala [1997] 1 WLR* in relation to a forfeiture by peaceable re-entry, although relief was granted upon terms. Both decisions were confirmed in *Sharples v Places for People Homes [2011] EWCA Civ 813*, and moreover extended in scope to Debt Relief Orders.

However, it should be noted that these cases permit *only* forfeiture; claims to recover arrears of rent on which the forfeiture is based (and presumably any interest due) would be subject to stay, and would require leave to issue in the first place.

Disapplication of s.146

A landlord's right to forfeit is unaffected by *s.146, Law of Property Act 1925* in certain instances of bankruptcy, pursuant to the provisions of *s.146(9)* and *(10)*. 'Bankruptcy', under *s.205(1)(i)* of the 1925 Act, includes the liquidation of a company.

Under *s.146(9)*, *s.146* is disapplied where forfeiture is based upon the bankruptcy of the tenant, if the lease is of:

(a) Agricultural or pastoral land;

(b) Mines or minerals;

(c) A house used or intended to be used as a public-house or beershop;

(d) A house let as dwelling-house, with the use of any furniture, books, works of art, or other chattels not being in the nature of fixtures; or

(e) Any property with respect to which the personal qualifications of the tenant are of importance for the preservation of the value

or character of the property, or on the ground of neigh-
bourhood to the landlord or to any person holding under him.

These are, presumably, all instances in which it is envisaged that significant harm might result to the landlord as a result of the tenant's
bankruptcy, if the landlord were to be unduly restricted or delayed in
the exercise of the right to forfeit. Since *s.146* does not apply in these
cases, the landlord is not required to serve a s.146 notice prior to forfeiture, or to wait a reasonable time, and there can be no application for
relief under *s.146(2)* or *s.146(4)*.

Under *s.146(10)*, as regards leases falling outside those classes specified
in *s.146(9)*, the provisions of *s.146* apply during the first year after
bankruptcy; if the lease is sold during that first year, they continue to
apply indefinitely. The purpose of this provision was explained in *Gee v
Harwood [1933] Ch 712* in terms of giving the insolvency practitioner a
sufficient breathing-space to realise the asset for the benefit of the creditors.

If here has been no sale of the lease for a year after bankruptcy, then
s.146 ceases to apply, and the landlord may forfeit without serving
notice and without any possibility of an application for relief. It will,
however, be a punctilious landlord indeed who has managed to avoid
waiving the right to forfeit for an entire year.

Individual Voluntary Arrangement

In the case of individual voluntary arrangements ('IVA's), where a
debtor intends to make a proposal for an arrangement with their creditors, and an application is made for an interim order for that purpose
under *s.253, Insolvency Act 1986*, a moratorium arises in relation to the
exercise of remedies against the debtor or their property. This applies
while the application is pending (*s.254*), and after the interim order has
been made (*s.252*). Following the meeting of creditors to vote on the
proposal, the insolvency practitioner must report to the court under
s.259 on the outcome of the meeting. If the proposal has been rejected,
the court may discharge any interim order, and the moratorium will

thereupon cease to apply. If the proposal has been accepted, the interim order will cease to have effect 28 days after the date of the report under *s.259*, and again the moratorium will come to an end.

While the moratorium lasts, by contrast to the position in relation to bankruptcy, it is comprehensive, and will prevent any forfeiture, by peaceable re-entry or court proceedings, without the leave of the court.

Once a proposal for an IVA has been approved by the requisite majority of creditors, it binds all creditors entitled to vote as if they had agreed to it, regardless of whether they voted in favour or against. The terms of the arrangement may well effectively modify the terms of the lease in some respects, and there will be more to say on this in relation to company voluntary arrangements (below).

The arrangement cannot, however, deprive the landlord of its propri-etary right to forfeit: *Discovery (Northampton) Ltd v Debenhams Retail Ltd [2019] EWHC 2441 (Ch)*. Therefore, where the lease provides for a right to forfeit in the event of an IVA being proposed, as it usually will, the terms of the arrangement cannot prevent forfeiture, and the approval of the proposal removes the restriction on it. Should forfeiture, post-approval of the IVA, be based upon arrears of rent, however, the landlord can only forfeit for non-payment of rent in the amount which is payable in accordance with the terms of the arrangement: *Thomas v Ken Thomas Ltd [2006] EWCA Civ 1504*.

LPA receivership

The appointment of a receiver of property under *ss.109-110, Law of Property Act 1925* does not restrict forfeiture (see below).

Insolvency of corporate tenant

Receivership

Where a borrower is in default under a loan agreement, the lender will generally have power under a mortgage or charge document to appoint a receiver of the property under *ss.109-110, Law of Property Act 1925*. This is known as an 'LPA receivership', and can occur in relation to both individual and corporate tenants. The other main type of receivership is 'administrative receivership', which applies only to corporate tenants. Administrative receivership is the process whereby the holder of a qualifying floating charge appoints an administrative receiver to realise the assets of a company that has breached the terms of the security agreement or debenture. Administrative receivership is infrequently encountered now, as it can only be used by creditors who hold a qualifying charge issued prior to 15th September 2003.

The essence of both types of receivership is a secured creditor taking steps to protect and realise its security. While the law recognises this as a desirable policy objective, the trend of insolvency law over recent decades has been towards rescue regimes of one sort or another, typically voluntary arrangements and administration. These, like liquidation and bankruptcy, are collective remedies, whereby all creditors' interests are taken into account. Receivership sits uneasily in this legislative context, and this is why holders of qualifying charges granted since 2003 are now restricted to the appointment of an administrator, instead of an administrative receiver.

It follows from the nature of receivership, as a remedy for only one, secured creditor, that there is no reason to restrict the remedies available to other creditors, including landlords. Hence there is no restriction on forfeiture where a tenant is in either form of receivership (see, for example, *Transag Haulage Ltd v Leyland DAF plc [1994] 2 BCLC 88* and *On Demand Information Plc v Michael Gershon (Finance) Plc [2000] EWCA Civ 251*).

Administration

The most common type of insolvency regime now encountered in relation to corporate tenants is administration. This is a rescue regime, and an administration order may be made in order to achieve any of a number of statutory purposes, the most common being the survival of the company's business as a going concern.

There are two ways in which a company can go into administration: (a) by a court order made at a formal hearing or (b) by certain parties lodging a series of prescribed documents at court (the 'out-of-court route').

(a) An application for a court order can be made by one or more creditors of the company, the company itself, its directors, a liquidator, a supervisor of a company voluntary arrangement, or under *s.359, Financial Services and Markets Act 2000* or *s.87A, Magistrates' Courts Act 1980*.

(b) Under the out-of-court route a company can be put into administration by filing at court a notice of appointment and certain specified supporting documents. This procedure may be commenced by either the company or its directors, or a qualifying floating charge holder (which is a party, usually a bank or other commercial lender, which has a floating charge that meets the requirements of *para. 14(2), Schedule B1, Insolvency Act 1986*).

Since administration could not achieve its purpose in the face of a free-for-all among creditors, all trying to enforce their claims, protection is given by means of an automatic moratorium. It is comprehensive in its effect, and prevents exercise of the right to forfeit arising as a result of the administration, unless with either the administrator's consent or the leave of the court (*para's 42, 43 and 44, Schedule B1, Insolvency Act 1986*). The moratorium begins immediately an administrator is appointed, by whichever route, and lasts for the duration of the administration.

Pre-pack administrations

A feature of recent years has been the development of the 'pre-pack administration'. This is the process by which a company is put into administration and its business or assets (or both) immediately sold under a sale which was negotiated with the involvement of an insolvency practitioner, but before their appointment as administrator. Often a pre-pack involves the sale of a company's business, together with its assets, on a going concern basis. Sometimes it will just involve the sale of some or all of the assets of the company. The rest of the company's assets or the business may be sold off in a separate pre-pack transaction, or the company may be put into liquidation.

Insolvency practitioners take the view that an off-market negotiation of this sort usually achieves a better outcome than marketing the business after an administrator has been appointed, while the appointment of an administrator just before the deal is signed off enables it to be implemented with protection from any creditors disappointed by its terms.

There are professional guidelines for insolvency practitioners that relate specifically to pre-packs. The Insolvency Service's *Statement of Insolvency Practice 16* ('*SIP 16*') was introduced in response to creditor concerns about pre-packs, principally a lack of accountability and transparency. It sets out a detailed list of the information which the administrator should disclose to creditors where there has been a pre-pack. To comply, an administrator should disclose to creditors, at the same time as the initial notice of appointment, or notice of intention to appoint, information including the price paid for the business/assets, and a description of other aspects of any wider transaction.

In practice, many firms of insolvency practitioners report to creditors within seven days of completing a pre-pack, setting out the required details. Although *SIP 16* is not legally binding, failure to comply with it could result in an administrator facing regulatory or disciplinary action. The Insolvency Service monitors the reporting by insolvency practitioners of pre-packs to creditors, with a view to ensuring compliance with *SIP 16*.

A pre-pack administration will invariably involve a breach of the alienation restrictions contained in any lease of premises which the purchaser of the business is going to occupy. The occupier must be a different legal entity from the tenant in administration, and since the deal is the result of an off-market negotiation, there will have been no request for landlord's consent to their occupation. Typically, a licence to occupy is granted, with the issue of landlord's consent to be dealt with later.

The landlord's ability to do anything about the breach is circumscribed by the moratorium. The key remedies are forfeiture of the lease, or an injunction to compel the tenant and the purchaser to terminate the licence to occupy or sub-lease, in reliance on *Crestfort Ltd v Tesco Stores Ltd [2005] 3 EGLR 25*.

Court's discretion

The court exercises its discretion as to the granting of leave in accordance with the principles laid down in *Re Atlantic Computer Systems plc [1992] 2 WLR 367*. Those guidelines, set out in the judgment of Nicholls LJ, are as follows:

- It is in every case for the person who seeks leave to persuade the court to grant leave.

- The moratorium is intended to assist the company, under the management of the administrators, to achieve the purpose for which the administration order was made. The court should normally allow the landlord to exercise his proprietary rights and repossess his land, if the repossession is unlikely to impede the achievement of that purpose.

- The court has to balance the legitimate interests of the landlord and the legitimate interests of the other creditors of the company (*Royal Trust Bank v Buchler [1989] BCLC 130*).

- In carrying out this balancing exercise, the court should give great weight to the proprietary interests of the landlord. So far as possible, the administration procedure should not be used to prejudice those who were secured creditors when the administration order was made in lieu of a winding-up order (*Bristol Airport plc v Powdrill [1990] Ch 744*). The same is true regarding the proprietary interests of a landlord. The administrator should not conduct a process for the benefit of unsecured creditors at the expense of those who have proprietary rights that they are seeking to exercise, save to the extent that this may be unavoidable. Even then, the court should attempt to limit the detriment suffered by the landlord.

- If a landlord stands to suffer significant loss from the prohibition on exercising his rights, the court should normally grant leave. For this purpose, loss comprises any kind of financial loss, direct or indirect, including loss because of delay, and may extend to loss that is not financial. However, if the general creditors are likely to suffer substantially greater loss by the grant of leave, or loss that is out of all proportion to the benefit which leave would confer on the landlord, that fact may outweigh the loss to the landlord caused by a refusal.

The discretion in practice

Three examples of the court's exercise of the discretion illustrate how these principles may be applied in practice.

- In *Innovate Logistics Limited (In Administration) v Sunberry Properties Limited, [2008] EWCA Civ 1261*, the tenant's administrator found a buyer for the business, and allowed them into occupation on a six-month licence, to enable the assets of the business to be moved (the premises were a cold storage facility, containing large quantities of stock which were to be sold for the benefit of the tenant's creditors). Under the terms of the licence, the buyer paid a monthly licence fee equal to the monthly rent under the lease and the administrator agreed to pay this on to the landlord. The licence to occupy was granted in breach of the terms of the lease, without landlord's consent. The landlord sought leave to apply for an injunction to terminate the licence to occupy.

  The Court of Appeal, conducting the balancing exercise referred to in the *Atlantic Computer Systems* guidelines, found that the only loss that the landlord would suffer would be the loss of interest on the rent that would normally have been paid quarterly in advance. The grant of a six-month licence to occupy would not confer any security of tenure on the purchaser, which would have to vacate at the end of the licence period. If the injunction were granted, not only would the landlord lose the benefit of the monthly rent, but the purpose of the administration would be frustrated because occupation of the premises by the purchaser was necessary to fulfil existing contracts of the insolvent tenant.

• The court must exercise its discretion afresh on each application for leave. In *Metro Nominees (Wandsworth) (No. 1) Ltd v Rayment (2008) BCC 40*, for example, the discretion was exercised to grant the landlord leave to issue proceedings for forfeiture, even though the administrator was proposing to pay for the accommodation. The administrators sold the business and assets on to a phoenix company, which was allowed into occupation without consulting the landlord. Permission to assign the lease was subsequently refused on the basis of the purchaser's lack of financial standing. The landlord sought leave to forfeit the lease, and the administrators claimed that they continued to require the premises for the purposes of the administration. Norris J held that the sale of the business had already taken place, so that the assignment would only benefit the purchaser. The tenant in administration no longer required the premises. Allowing the landlord to forfeit would therefore not impede the object of the administration.

• In *Re SSRL Realisations Ltd (in administration) [2015] EWHC 2590 (Ch)*, the tenant had entered into a pre-pack administration involving the sale of its business. As part of the deal, a licence to occupy the demised premises was granted to a wholly-owned subsidiary of the tenant, and the shares in the subsidiary were immediately thereafter sold to the purchaser. The grant of the licence was a breach of alienation covenant, and the landlord sought leave to forfeit.

The licence was intended as an interim measure pending formal consent being obtained to an assignment of the lease to the subsidiary. The purchaser had agreed to pay the tenant in administration a substantial sum for the assignment of the lease to the subsidiary, if landlord's consent could be obtained. The administrator therefore argued that forfeiture would result in the loss of a valuable asset, and so impede the purpose of the administration, while at the same time it would confer a very considerable windfall benefit on the landlord.

However, the landlord opposed the assignment on the basis that both the subsidiary and the purchaser were of insufficient financial standing, and on the facts this was found to be reasonable.

The court held that whether the lease in fact had substantial value depended on *"the prospect that [the administrators] will be able to find some other, as yet unidentified, assignee which is prepared to pay a premium for the lease and to which [the landlord] cannot reasonably withhold consent to assign"*. On the available evidence the premises were more likely to require a rent-free period than command a premium, and leave to forfeit was granted.

Compulsory liquidation

Compulsory liquidation is the winding-up of the tenant company and distribution of its assets on the ground of its inability to pay its debts as they fall due. The disapplication of *s.146, Law of Property Act 1925* in certain instances of bankruptcy, under *s.146(9)* and *(10)*, considered above, extends to liquidation. In those instances, therefore, no s.146 notice need be served, and relief from forfeiture would not be available. The following restrictions, however, would still apply.

In the case of liquidation, after a winding-up petition has been presented, but before a winding-up order is made, any pending *"action or proceeding"* against the company may be stayed or restrained by the relevant court under *s.126, Insolvency Act 1986*. That clearly applies to forfeiture by court proceedings, but it is less clear whether it applies to peaceable re-entry, since *"action"* is not defined in the Act. It was held in *Re Memco Engineering Ltd [1986] Ch 86* that distress for rent was an "*action or proceeding*", and it is perhaps likely that peaceable re-entry, being another extra-judicial, self-help remedy, would be regarded in the same way.

Once a winding-up order has been made, or a provisional liquidator appointed, "*no action or proceeding shall be proceeded with or commenced against the company or its property, except by leave of the court and subject to such terms as the court may impose*" (*s.130(2)*). Thus, as in the case of administration, issuing proceedings for forfeiture would require the leave of the court, and equally the court may exercise its discretion to lift any stay of such proceedings made previously. Under *s.130(2)* the same doubt applies as under *s.126*, as to whether peaceable re-entry is an "*action or proceeding*".

Blue Jeans orders

Where leave of the court is required in order to forfeit, there is a con-venient procedure following *Re Blue Jeans Sales Ltd [1979] 1 All ER 641*, whereby the court, when granting leave to forfeit, can at the same hearing make an order for possession. The circumstances in which such orders have been made, at least in reported cases (e.g. *Re National Jazz Centre Ltd [1988] 2 EGLR 57*) are those of undisputed arrears of rent, where there could be no defence to the action. This is a useful short-cut in straightforward cases.

There is no technical reason why this short-cut should not be available where leave is required in an administration as well. Anecdotally, Blue Jeans orders have been obtained against tenants in administration, though so far as is known, not in a disputed or a reported case. If an administrator resists forfeiture, then clearly the question whether leave should be granted may not be shortly resolved.

In *Re Blue Jeans Sales*, there were sub-tenants in occupation, and as they were not party to the winding-up proceedings, nor could they be, there was an issue as to how they could be protected. The court held that they were protected by the court's rules, the relevant provision at that time being *Rules of the Supreme Court, Ord. 45, r.3*. There is equivalent provision under the current *Civil Procedure Rules*: a writ of possession to enforce the order cannot be issued without the court's permission, under *CPR 83.13(2)*, and under *CPR 83.13(8)(a)* permission will not be granted unless is it shown:

> "*that every person in actual possession of the whole or any part of the land ('the occupant') has received such notice of the proceedings as appears to the court sufficient to enable the occupant to apply to the court for any relief to which the occupant may be entitled*".

In a case where a Blue Jeans order is made, relief from forfeiture may be applied for in the insolvency proceedings: *Re Brompton Securities Ltd [No 2] [1988] 3 All ER 677*.

Rent as an expense of the insolvency

While a landlord may be refused leave to forfeit, the flipside to that coin is that rent will usually be paid during the period that the property is used for the purposes of the insolvency, either by agreement with the insolvency practitioner, or by court order on the basis that it is an expense of the insolvency. This is of considerable practical importance to landlords; if rent is payable as an expense, it sits near the top of the priority order for the distribution of the tenant's assets, and will usually be paid in full. Otherwise, it is among the unsecured debts, and the landlord will have to wait for whatever dividend is ultimately payable.

Insolvency law recognises a general principle that the costs of the insolvency procedure should be borne by those for whose benefit the procedure is carried out, namely the creditors. Those costs should therefore be paid in priority to the claims of the creditors. So, if an insolvency office-holder uses leasehold premises for the purpose of the insolvency, that use should be paid for in priority, particularly since landlords' remedies are restricted by the insolvency.

However, because rent is regarded as having been incurred as a future debt at the time the lease was executed, the starting-point is that both elements of rent are regarded as unsecured claims, and not as an expense of the insolvency.

In liquidations, this problem was circumvented by the approach taken in *Re Lundy Granite (1870-71) LR 6 Ch App 462*, whereby if a debtor company uses leasehold premises for the purposes of the liquidation, and so denies the landlord its proprietary rights, the sums falling due under the lease must be paid in full. The sums are treated as if they were liquidation expenses, and this approach hardened into a rigid principle, independent of the legislation setting out what was payable as a liquidation expense.

In relation to the administration procedure, the issue came up for consideration in *Re Atlantic Computer Systems plc [1992] 2 WLR 367*, where the Court of Appeal took the view that given the different objectives of administration, as compared to liquidation, there was no place for any rigid principle along *Lundy Granite* lines, although the *Lundy Granite* approach would be among the factors to be considered. There was a discretion whose exercise would reflect the wider range of factual circumstances in administrations. Payment of apportioned sums to reflect the actual period of use by the administrators could be ordered.

This approach came to be doubted, in the wake of some technical amendments to the *Insolvency Rules*, in a line of cases beginning with *Re Toshoku Finance UK plc [2002] UKHL 6*, and ending with *Goldacre (Offices) Ltd v Nortel Networks UK Ltd [2010] Ch 455*, and *Leisure (Norwich) II Ltd v Luminar Lava Ignite Ltd [2012] BCC 497*. It is unnecessary to consider those cases, however, in the light of the Court of Appeal's consideration of the issue in *Pillar Denton Ltd v Jervis [2014] EWCA 180*. As a consequence of that decision, the correct principle is that an administrator or liquidator must make payments at the rate of the rent for the duration of any period during which it retains possession for the benefit of the insolvency process, the rent accruing from day to day. Those sums are payable as an expense of the administration or liquidation. The duration of the possession period is a question of fact and is not determined by reference to rent payment days.

The test for payment of rent as an expense of the insolvency is whether the office-holder is making beneficial use of the premises, which includes trading, storage or marketing the premises.

Where rent is payable as an expense, although this means the landlord will get paid, it should not be assumed that the rent will be paid against quarterly demands as if there were no insolvency. The office-holder is unlikely to pay a full quarter in advance unless the beneficial use is certain to continue for the whole quarter. There will probably be an attempt to negotiate payment in arrears on a monthly, weekly or even daily basis. Another possibility is payment of rent into a blocked account, or joint account with the landlord, to be released at appropriate intervals.

Company Voluntary Arrangement

A company voluntary arrangement ('CVA'), like an individual voluntary arrangement, is an arrangement between a company and its creditors, proposed and then supervised by an insolvency practitioner, and sanctioned by the court. A CVA is normally proposed by the company's directors, but can be proposed by its administrator or liquidator. The aim is generally a compromise in satisfaction of its debts, or a scheme of arrangement of its affairs.

When CVAs were first introduced it was envisaged that they would principally be used for simple arrangements by small companies, however, they have come to be a favoured vehicle for major multiple retailers.

The essence of the procedure is that an insolvency practitioner is appointed as 'nominee' to propose a scheme of arrangement, the content of which is extremely flexible, since the term is not defined in the legislation. It may not affect the rights of a secured creditor to enforce their security, and may not impose entirely new obligations (as opposed to restricting or altering existing ones), but is otherwise unrestricted.

As in the case of an IVA, the proposal is put to a meeting of creditors, and if approved by 75% by value of the creditors, it becomes binding as if it were a contract entered into between the company and its creditors, including any who may not have voted in favour of it.

It might be expected that an effective restructuring would be very wide in its scope, covering equity and debt raising, changes to management and supply contracts and so forth. However, it has become common-place now for multiple retailers to propose CVAs which simply address the retailer's lease liabilities, usually by means of closing stores and cutting rents. These are sometimes called 'landlord CVAs'.

Typically, a CVA proposal will place stores into a number of categories, including at least:

- Profitable stores, where no adverse impact on the landlords is pro-posed;

- Stores in difficulties, where the proposal is likely to include rent reductions or a move to turnover rent; and

- Loss-making stores, to be closed altogether.

There is no moratorium against enforcement action in the case of a CVA, unless it is a small company. A small company is defined as one that satisfies at least two of the conditions set out in *s.247, Companies Act 1985*:

- Turnover of not more than £2.8m;

- Balance sheet of not more than £1.4m;

- Not more than 50 employees.

In the case of a small company, a moratorium arises upon the present-ation of the proposal, and lasts for 28 days, up to the creditors' meeting.

It can be extended by application to the court up to a maximum of two months. Its effect will be to prevent forfeiture, by whatever method, unless with the leave of the court (*para.12, Sched A1, part II, Insolvency Act 1986*).

Though there is no statutory moratorium applying otherwise, landlord CVAs of the type described often include a contractual moratorium, preventing landlords from exercising their remedies.

When a major retailer proposes a landlord CVA, the insolvency practitioner will generally approach the British Property Federation's Insolvency Committee. It will engage with the insolvency practitioner in relation to the fairness of the terms proposed. The benefit to the retailer and the insolvency practitioner is that the outcome of the process is likely to be fewer landlords voting against the proposals at the creditors' meeting. Some high-profile CVA proposals have been defeated by landlords voting to reject them.

If a CVA is approved, it remains open to landlords to challenge it on the basis of unfair prejudice, and such challenges have on occasion been successful (e.g. *Mourant & Co Trustees Ltd v Sixty UK Ltd (in liquidation) [2010] EWHC 1890 (Ch)*).

A number of issues as to the permissible scope of a CVA, and unfair prejudice, were addressed in *Discovery (Northampton) Ltd v Debenhams Retail Ltd [2019] EWHC 2441 (Ch)*. In that case, the terms of the Debenhams Retail CVA included a reduction of the rent payable to various landlords of Debenhams stores, and removal from the leases of the landlords' right to forfeit. The landlords challenged the CVA on a number of grounds:

- Future rent is not a debt and so the landlords are not creditors, such that the CVA cannot bind them. This was rejected: the definition of debt is broad enough to include pecuniary contingent liabilities, such as future rent.

- A CVA cannot operate to reduce rent payable under leases: it is automatically unfairly prejudicial. This too was rejected. CVAs modify obligations, and modifying the obligation to pay rent is not prima facie unfair.

- The CVA treated the landlords less favourably than other unsecured creditors without any proper justification. The court considered that treating the landlords differently was necessary to secure the continuation of the company's business, which was a sufficient justification.

- The right to forfeiture is a proprietary right that cannot be altered by a CVA. This ground of challenge succeeded. The right of re-entry is property belonging to the landlord. The attempt to rewrite the lease in this respect went beyond the jurisdiction conferred by the *Insolvency Act 1986*.

The finding on this final point essentially lifts any contractual moratorium which purports to extend to forfeiture. The applicant landlords in the case were not disposed to forfeit, but in other cases companies will be exposed to the risk of losing premises with some value.

As was noted in relation to IVAs, forfeiture based upon arrears of rent, following approval of an IVA, can only be based upon non-payment of rent in the amount which is payable in accordance with the terms of the arrangement: *Thomas v Ken Thomas Ltd [2006] EWCA Civ 1504*.

Summary

As regards individual tenants:

- The presentation of a bankruptcy petition, or the making of a bankruptcy order, do not prevent forfeiture, whether by peaceable re-entry or court proceedings. However, the landlord may only forfeit, and not claim any debts due under the lease.

- In certain limited instances of forfeiture based upon the tenant's bankruptcy, s.146, Law of Property Act 1925 does not apply.

- As regards individual voluntary arrangements, an interim moratorium applies pending the creditors' meeting, which will prevent forfeiture without the leave of the court. Once an IVA is approved that moratorium falls away, and the terms of the IVA may not deprive the landlord of the ability to forfeit.

- Appointment of an LPA receiver does not restrict forfeiture.

As regards corporate tenants:

- Neither the appointment of an LPA receiver nor that of an administrative receiver restricts forfeiture.

- Appointment of an administrator imposes a moratorium which prevents forfeiture unless with the administrator's consent or the leave of the court. The discretion whether to grant leave is exercised in accordance with principles which recognise the importance of the landlord's proprietary right of forfeiture, but prevent its exercise if it would impede the purpose of the administration.

- In certain limited instances of forfeiture based upon the tenant's liquidation, s.146, Law of Property Act 1925 does not apply.

- Prior to the making of a winding-up order actions or proceedings against the company, including forfeiture proceedings, may be stayed. Once a winding-up order has been made, or a provisional liquidator appointed, no action or proceeding may be commenced or progressed without the leave of the court. It is not clear whether peaceable re-entry is an 'action or proceeding' for these purposes.

- An administrator or liquidator must make payments at the rate of the rent for the duration of any period during which it retains possession for the benefit of the insolvency process, the rent accruing from day to day. Those sums are payable as an expense of the administration or liquidation.

- A company voluntary arrangement in relation to a small company will impose a moratorium, pending the creditors' meeting, which prevents forfeiture without the leave of the court. Once a CVA is approved any statutory moratorium falls away, though the terms of the CVA may include a contractual moratorium. However, the terms of the CVA may not deprive the landlord of the ability to forfeit.

CHAPTER TWELVE
PROPOSALS FOR RE-CASTING
THE LAW

This chapter summarises the Law Commission's proposals for replacement of the law of forfeiture by a new statutory scheme.

The reader who has progressed this far may, it is hoped, have found this account of the present law of forfeiture not only of practical assistance but also of some interest. Feudal survivals such as 'denial of title' are at least picturesque, and while the legal profession is not an obvious career choice for the seeker of excitement, dawn raids to change the locks on a property have a certain swashbuckling appeal, perhaps the more so for being stigmatised as "*dubious and dangerous*" by senior members of the judiciary. One suspects, however, that the principal reaction will have been a growing sense of wonder at the survival of such an idiosyncratic body of law.

A law in need of re-casting

We noted at the outset that the Law Commission has made proposals to reshape the law in this area radically, and it is a measure of how problematic are central features of the law of forfeiture that the Commission concluded that reform of the existing law would be inadequate. We have used the word 're-casting' instead, as a better description of what is proposed, namely replacement of the existing law in its entirety by a completely new statutory scheme.

As the Commission's final Report says:

"… *the time for piecemeal reform has passed and … the case for the implementation of a modern statute governing all aspects of termination for breach of covenant is overwhelming*".

The proposals, incorporating a draft *Landlord and Tenant (Termination of Tenancies) Bill*, have a long history. The Commission's first *Report on the Forfeiture of Tenancies (Law Com no.142)*, itself building on work going back to 1968, was published in 1985. It was followed in 1994 by publication of the draft Bill (*Law Com no. 221*). A further consultation took place in 2004, and a final report, incorporating an amended version of the draft Bill, was published in October 2006 (*Law Com no. 303*).

Technical, non-urgent measures of this sort always take their time to reach the top of the in-tray, but in March 2019 the report of the Ministry of Housing, Communities and Local Government on leasehold reform recommended that the government should immediately take up the Law Commission's proposals in relation to the law of forfeiture.

At the time of writing, government remains much occupied with Britain's departure from the European Union and its consequences, and this is likely to be the case for some time. It is nevertheless very much to be hoped that time can be found to implement these proposals, the sooner the better.

Problems with the present law

The Law Commission has identified a range of problems with the law as it stands, and they should have been apparent from the preceding chapters of this book. When one lists them together, the need for change becomes obvious:

(a) It is unnecessary and anachronistic that a landlord should be entitled to forfeit a tenancy purely on the ground that the tenant has denied the landlord's title.

(b) The law concerning formal demands for rent is obsolete.

(c) The distinction between rent and non-rent breaches is unnecessary and complicating.

(d) The operation of the doctrine of waiver is a trap for landlords. It is not easy, and not always possible, to avoid waiving the right to forfeit, and the steps required in attempting to do so stand in the way of settlement discussions.

(e) The distinction between continuing and once-and-for-all breaches is a further unnecessary complication.

(f) The multiplicity of jurisdictions for the granting of relief from forfeiture is unnecessary and confusing, and the applicable rules cause problems for a landlord in re-letting the premises after forfeiture.

(g) The provisions in *s.146(8)-(10), Law of Property Act 1925*, denying tenants the right to claim relief from forfeiture by statute in certain exceptional circumstances, now appear to be anomalous and unnecessary.

(h) The circumstances in which the court may grant relief from forfeiture are not sufficiently certain. The distinction between remediable and irremediable breaches is unsatisfactory, confused and unnecessary.

(i) A landlord may suffer injustice as a result of the rule that relief from forfeiture follows upon the remedying of a breach of covenant. It should be possible for the landlord to recover possession where the tenant has been persistently late in paying rent or has been responsible for persistent breaches of obligation.

(j) A tenant may suffer injustice as a result of the rule that a breach of covenant which casts a 'stigma' on the premises cannot be remedied, and so is highly likely to lead to a refusal of relief by the court.

(k) In general, the rules concerning sub-tenants, mortgagees and others holding derivative interests in the tenancy confer insufficient protection on those parties. This can lead not only to the uncompensated loss of occupational, security or other rights but also to extremely late applications for relief from holders of derivative interests. This may be prejudicial to the landlord who has forfeited, particularly if the property has been re-let in the meantime.

(l) The ability for a landlord to forfeit a lease by peaceable re-entry where the tenant has gone into bankruptcy is anomalous and potentially puts other creditors at a serious disadvantage.

The Commission is to be congratulated on its achievement of devising a replacement for the remedy of forfeiture which effectively addresses all these problems, while recognisably retaining the useful features of the present law. Moreover, it is a set of proposals which has generally been warmly welcomed by professional advisers, landlords, tenants and lenders.

The proposed new scheme

It is proposed that the existing law of forfeiture be abolished. The new scheme would apply instead to all leases, whether entered into before or after the scheme commencement.

<u>Pre-requisites of termination under the scheme</u>

Like the existing law, the scheme's starting point is tenant default, but where the existing law relies upon the drafting of the individual lease to identify tenant default, under the new scheme it is given a statutory definition. It follows that post-commencement leases need not contain any forfeiture clause. The right to terminate in the event of tenant default will be a statutory one, not contractual. "Tenant default" is defined as:

- Breach of any covenant of the lease, including

    o Express covenants

- ○ Implied covenants

- ○ Covenants imposed by law

- ○ Circumstances arising out of the tenant's conduct (e.g. insolvency) in which the lease provides for automatic termination

• Where there has been an unlawful assignment, breach of covenant by the previous tenant (thus enabling action to be taken against the unlawful assignee)

• Breach of covenant by a guarantor.

In the case of a post-commencement lease, the parties might by agreement exclude the operation of the scheme in relation to specific covenants ("excepted covenants"). Breach of an excepted covenant would not be "tenant default", and would not engage the scheme.

In the case of a pre-commencement lease, breach of covenant will only be considered "tenant default" if it would have entitled the landlord to forfeit under the existing law. Once the scheme has commenced, that right to forfeit will no longer be exercisable; instead the breach will entitle the landlord to take action under the scheme.

The absence of a forfeiture clause in a post-commencement lease might mean that tenants would not appreciate the possible consequences of a breach of covenant. Therefore, there would be a requirement in such cases for the landlord to provide the tenant with an explanatory statement, in prescribed form, explaining the landlord's right to terminate the lease in the event of tenant default. The expectation would be that this would be done at the time the lease was entered into, though that would not be a requirement. It would at any rate have to be done before any enforcement action, as the landlord would not be able to terminate the lease under the scheme unless an explanatory statement had been provided, although the court would have power to dispense with the need for a statement in appropriate cases.

No such statement would be required in relation to pre-commencement leases.

Alternative termination procedures

Just as the present law permits forfeiture either by court proceedings or by peaceable re-entry, so the new scheme would provide for termination through the court, while also permitting termination without recourse to the court in certain circumstances. The two procedures are referred to collectively as "termination action".

Proceeding by way of court action is referred to as a "termination claim", and that procedure is commenced by service of a "tenant default notice"; the non-court option is called the "summary termination procedure", and is commenced by a "summary termination notice". The landlord would have to decide which procedure to adopt, since they could not run concurrently.

They could, however, run consecutively: under the scheme, once the landlord has served a tenant default notice specifying a tenant default, they may not serve a summary termination notice specifying the same default, unless the tenant default notice is withdrawn, or the termination claim is dismissed or abandoned. Equally, once the landlord has served a summary termination notice specifying a tenant default, they may not serve a tenant default notice specifying the same default, unless the summary termination notice is withdrawn or discharged by order of the court.

While a landlord at present has an almost completely free choice as to which method of forfeiture to adopt, the summary termination procedure under the new scheme would be available only in very restricted circumstances (see below).

Default period

Whichever type of termination action is adopted, the tenant default notice or summary termination notice would have to be served within a "default period" of six months after (a) the day on which the landlord first knew that the facts constituting the tenant default had occurred, or (b) in the case of a continuing breach, any day on which the landlord knew those facts were continuing to occur. The period might be extended by agreement between the parties.

This mechanism stands in for the doctrine of waiver in the current law of forfeiture. It performs the same function of requiring the landlord to decide whether the tenant default is sufficiently serious that action is required, and allows a generous period in which to do so. Since the lease is not immediately terminated by service of a tenant default notice or a summary termination notice, there is no need to require an irrevocable decision at an early stage of events, nor is there any incongruity between the landlord (a) serving the notice, and (b) continuing to demand and accept rent, and otherwise behaving in all respects consistently with the continued existence of the lease.

Certain aspects of the law of waiver would apparently continue to have relevance. The degree of knowledge required to start the default period running would be the same, and the imputed knowledge of the landlord's agent would continue to be sufficient. It would continue to be relevant to identify continuing breaches as a separate category.

Recipients of notice

Putting right an obvious inadequacy in the present law, under the new scheme a tenant default notice or summary termination notice would have to be served upon, not only the tenant, but also holders of "qualifying interests", principally sub-tenants, mortgagees and chargees.

The requirement would be limited to those qualifying interest-holders of which the landlord had knowledge. As well as actual knowledge, landlords will be deemed to have knowledge of a qualifying interest if they have been notified of it in writing, or if it is registered at the Land Registry, the local land charges register, or the register of charges kept by the Registrar of Companies.

Where the tenant default was an unlawful assignment, the notice would have to be served upon the assignee, rather than the assignor.

Under either procedure, the notice would also have to be served at the demised premises, addressed to "The Occupier".

Termination claim

Tenant default notice

The tenant default notice, in prescribed form, would set out the details of the specific tenant default, and also any response that the landlord seeks from the tenant: that might be remedy of the default, or it might be payment of financial compensation. It might be that the landlord simply wants to terminate the lease, and does not require any remedial action. It might also be that the default complained of is irremediable (though it is not the intention that the existing law's distinction between remediable and irremediable breaches should be preserved). If remedial action is required, the notice must specify a deadline by which it should be completed; it must be a reasonable deadline, and may not be less than seven days after the notice has been given.

The intention is that the notice will provide a breathing-space for negotiation. Because the present rules on waiver would not apply, of course, negotiation would be possible without any risk of waiving the right to forfeit. The expectation is that parties would take advantage of alternative dispute resolution mechanisms, and that many if not most issues would be settled without the need to commence a termination claim.

A landlord would not be able to make a termination claim unless the requirements as to service of a tenant default notice had been complied with, and the deadline for any remedial action specified in the notice had expired without the action being taken. The court would, however, have power to dispense with service of a tenant default notice, or any of the requirements as to its content, if just and equitable to do so. The tenant would be secure in the knowledge that no termination claim could be made up to the expiry of the deadline.

While a notice would not be rendered invalid by the landlord having stipulated an unreasonably short time for completing any remedial action specified, the length of time given would be taken into account by the court in deciding upon the termination claim. Equally the court could take into account the landlord having specified some unreasonable or disproportionate remedial action, or having specified no remedial action at all.

Court's discretion

A range of orders will be available to the court. The landlord will in every case seek a termination order, usually coupled with an order for possession (though not invariably; the landlord may, for example, have granted possession to a third party by then). However, one of the other available orders may be acceptable to the landlord, and the landlord might include a statement to that effect in their statement of case.

The court will be required to make such order as it thinks appropriate and proportionate in the circumstances. In exercising its discretion, the court will be required to take into account a statutory list of factors:

(a) The conduct of the parties

(b) The nature and terms of any qualifying interest in the tenancy and the circumstances in which it was granted

(c) The extent to which action to remedy the default is possible, or has been taken

(d) The reasonableness of any deadline specified in the tenant default notice

(e) The extent to which the tenant has complied, or would be likely to comply, with any remedial order made in respect of the default

(f) Any other remedy available to the landlord

(g) Any other matter thought to be relevant.

The range of orders available to the court is not circumscribed. The discretion is as wide as it can possibly be. However, the scheme does specify six types of order in particular. Conditions may be imposed upon the grant of any order, such as payment of any sums owed, or provision of security for performance in future. The six specified orders are:

1. A "termination order", as the name suggests, terminates the lease, together with any interests derived from it. It will specify a termination date, and may order possession to be given up on the same date. Subject to any appeal, the order is final, with no possibility of a late application for 'relief', as there is under the present law.

2. A "remedial order", requiring the tenant to take action to remedy the default, by a specified date. At that date, if the required action has not been taken, the landlord's termination claim is stayed for a three-month period. The landlord may apply within that period for the stay to be lifted, and if it is, a termination order may result. If the application to lift the stay is unsuccessful, the termination claim comes to an end. If the landlord fails to apply to lift the stay, the termination claim automatically comes to an end at the end of the three months.

3. An "order for sale" may require the lease to be sold, and the proceeds distributed. A receiver will be appointed by the court to carry out the sale. Unless the court directs otherwise, the proceeds will be used to pay first the receiver's costs, then any sum owing to the landlord by reason of the tenant default, and then any sum secured by a qualifying interest in the lease (i.e. a mortgage or charge). Any money left over will be paid to the tenant. The lease will be sold subject to any pre-existing interests such as sub-leases.

   The court could not order the lease to be sold in breach of a covenant against assignment without the landlord's consent. Where (as is almost always the case) consent is not to be unreasonably withheld, the court could nevertheless order sale if satisfied that it would be unreasonable for the landlord not to consent. Similarly, where any charge over the lease contained a covenant not to assign, no order for sale could be made without the chargee's consent.

4. A "transfer order" would only be available to the holder of a qual-ifying interest, and would require the transfer of the lease to the applicant, or a nominated third party such as a management company. Similar restrictions would apply as in the case of an order for sale.

5. A "new tenancy order" would also would only be available to the holder of a qualifying interest, and would require the grant of a new lease to the applicant of all or part of the demised premises. This would have the effect of terminating the original lease, together with all pre-existing derivative interests. The terms would be determined by the court in default of agreement between the parties, and the court could additionally order the grant of new derivative rights equivalent to any terminated.

6. Finally, a "joint tenancy adjustment order" would be available where the lease was held by joint tenants. This would provide that one or more of the joint tenants should cease to be a tenant from a specified date. This might be sought where not all of the joint tenants wish to contest the termination claim.

The available range of orders, coupled with the list of discretionary factors, replaces the confused patchwork of relief jurisdictions with a principled and flexible scheme.

Qualifying interest-holders

Qualifying interests are not only sub-leases and mortgages, but also charges (both legal and equitable), options to purchase and rights of pre-emption in respect of the lease and any sub-leases, rights to an assignment of the whole or part of the premises, or to an assignment of a charge, and any right to an overriding lease under the *Landlord and Tenant (Covenants) Act 1995*. Thus, the scheme expands the class of those protected, and gives clarity and certainty.

Any holder of such an interest may respond to the landlord's termination action, whether or not the tenant has done so, by applying to the court for any order other than a termination order.

<u>Summary termination procedure</u>

The summary termination procedure is intended to provide a quicker and cheaper means of termination, but in restricted circumstances. It will be available following tenant default, in circumstances where, if a termination claim were made, the tenant would have no realistic prospect of resisting a termination order, and there is no other reason why a trial of that claim should take place.

That is a deliberately high bar; it is expected that summary termination will only be used where the premises have been abandoned or the tenant is impecunious, with no hope of remedying the breach for which the landlord is seeking to forfeit. The scope for using the remedy is very much narrower than the availability of peaceable re-entry, under the present law.

The procedure is commenced by the landlord serving a summary termination notice. There are further restrictions, providing that a summary termination notice cannot be served:

• Where a person is lawfully residing in the premises

• Where there is more than 25 years of the lease term unexpired

• Where the lease (other than an agricultural tenancy) was granted for seven years or more, three years or more of the term remains unexpired, and the default complained of is breach of repairing covenant (this restriction effectively reproduces the limitations imposed by the *Leasehold Property (Repairs) Act 1938*)

- Where a post-commencement tenancy provides that the summary termination procedure may not be used in relation to the specific breach of covenant

- Where a pre-commencement tenancy does not entitle the landlord to forfeit by peaceable re-entry in relation to the specific breach of covenant.

The summary termination notice must be in prescribed form, and cannot require the tenant to remedy the default (if remedial action is required, the appropriate course is to serve a tenant default notice). Instead, it is a termination notice, which will have the effect of terminating the lease one month after service. That can be prevented by the tenant or any qualifying interest-holder applying to discharge the notice. If such an application is made, the termination will only take effect upon dismissal of the application.

A potential problem here is that the landlord may not know straight away that the tenant has applied for a discharge order. It may take several weeks for the application to be processed by the court and served on the landlord. In the meantime, the landlord is left in a state of uncertainty and unable to retake possession. Perhaps a requirement for the tenant to serve notice on the landlord that they have lodged an application at court would be a useful tweak to the procedure.

If an application is made for a discharge order, there is a statutory presumption in favour of discharge, which the landlord could only displace by showing (a) that there was no realistic prospect of the applicant resisting a termination order, and (b) that there was no other reason why the matter should be resolved by way of a hearing of a termination claim. That means that discharge would be the usual outcome.

The landlord might then serve a tenant default notice with a view to making a termination claim. There is a risk that the default period might have expired by then, though the court would have a discretion to dispense with the requirement to serve a tenant default notice within the default period, if just and equitable to do so. However, this would be a risk of adopting the summary termination procedure, and another reason why it is likely to be little-used. That is, of course, the intention.

The present ability to apply for relief following forfeiture would be reproduced, following use of the summary termination procedure. An application by the former tenant, or a former qualifying interest-holder, would be possible within six months after termination by this means. The court could make any order which it considered appropriate and proportionate, such as the grant of a new lease to the applicant, or the payment of compensation, but could not retrospectively revive the terminated tenancy.

Special cases

- Subject to contrary provision in the lease, a covenant to pay rent will be treated as broken if payment is not made within 21 days of the due date. Formal demand will be unnecessary.

- The protections for long leaseholders of dwellings contained in the *Commonhold and Leasehold Reform Act 2002* are retained.

- Also retained are the protections provided for in the *Leasehold Property (Repairs) Act 1938*, by means of restricting the court's ability to make orders in circumstances where the Act would apply.

- The scheme would remove the ability for the landlord to peaceably re-enter in the event of the tenant's bankruptcy, and otherwise preserve the various restrictions and protections afforded in the various insolvency procedures.

Conclusion

The central idea of forfeiture, as observed in the Foreword, is the simple one that if the tenant breaches their lease obligations, then the landlord has the right to terminate the lease. There is nothing unreasonable or draconian about that, and termination should be an available remedy under the law, provided that the tenant has the opportunity to prevent termination by remedying the breach, provided further that termination is not disproportionate, and provided finally that third parties with relevant property interests in the lease can be properly protected. In its own eccentric way, that is what the law of forfeiture has been trying to achieve for centuries.

The Law Commission's proposed scheme draws on the good aspects of the present law while learning the lessons of the bad. It is modern, coherent and would enable the courts to do justice as between all the potential interested parties. It should be implemented without further delay.

Summary

The Law Commission has proposed two forms of statutory termination to replace forfeiture: first, a court-based termination claim; and, secondly, an accelerated process to replace peaceable re-entry (the summary termination procedure). A landlord must decide which to use, and the tenancy continues until the court makes a termination order or a summary termination takes effect. The statutory scheme would apply to all tenancies, whether entered into before or after the scheme comes into force and whether or not they contain a forfeiture clause.

Termination claim

Under the standard procedure a landlord must serve a "tenant default notice" within six months of the tenant's default and not less than seven days before bringing a termination claim.

The notice must be served on the tenant and all derivative interest holders, specifying what needs to be done to remedy the breach and by when. Where the breach is not remedied or an agreement reached, the landlord can begin an action at court. If the court is satisfied that the tenant default has occurred, it has the discretion to make a range of different orders, including a termination order to end the tenancy or an order requiring the tenant to remedy the breach, although there are a number of specific considerations (for example, the parties' conduct) that must be taken into account.

Summary termination procedure

The proposed summary termination procedure will allow a landlord to bring a tenancy to an end without applying to court.

A landlord must first serve a "summary termination notice" on the tenant and derivative interest holders. This will end the tenancy one month from the date of service, unless the tenant or a derivative interest holder applies to court to discharge the notice. If no application is made in that time, the landlord may take back possession. If an application is made for a discharge order, the tenancy will only determine if and when the application is refused.

A landlord will only be able to defeat a discharge application by showing that the tenant would, in standard termination proceedings, have no realistic prospect of persuading the court not to make a termination order, and there is no other reason why the matter should be disposed of by way of termination claim.

The former tenant or a former derivative interest holder would be able to apply to court for a "post-termination order" within six months after summary termination.

APPENDIX
SAMPLE S.146 NOTICE AND PARTICULARS OF CLAIM

The following example s.146 notice and Particulars of Claim are provided for illustrative purposes. They are not intended as precedents, and should not be used as such.

The scenario on which they are based is as follows:

- *Beale Investments Ltd owns the freehold of a lock-up shop at 6 Albert Square, Walford, East London. The shop was let on 24 April 2017 to Phillip Mitchell, trading as Phil's Tracksuits, for a term of ten years from the date of execution of the lease at the annual rent of £15,000 subject to five-yearly upward-only rent review.*

- *The lease restricted the use of the shop to the sale of sports goods. It also contained a comprehensive alienation clause prohibiting assignment, sub-letting, and parting with or sharing occupation or possession of the premises, in part or whole, without landlord's written prior consent.*

- *The rent due on 29 September 2019 was not paid, and on 15 October 2019 Mr Beale of Beale Investments Ltd visited the premises hoping to discuss this with Mr Mitchell. He found that the trading style had changed from Phil's Tracksuits to Fowler's Flowers, and that a florist's business was being carried on there. An assistant, Katherine Slater, said that the business owner was a Martin Fowler, who was not present at that time.*

- *Mr Beale sees this as an opportunity to recover possession and re-let at a higher rent, to a better tenant.*

Example s.146 Notice

Notice under section 146, Law of Property Act 1925

TO: Phillip Mitchell of [address] ("the Tenant") and
Martin Fowler of [address] ("the Occupier")[1]

FROM: Beale Investments Ltd of [address] ("the Landlord")

This Notice is given in relation to a Lease of 6 Albert Square, Walford,
London E20 ("the Demised Premises") dated 24 April 2017 and made
between (1) the Landlord and (2) the Tenant ("the Lease").[2]

1. The reversion immediately expectant upon the Lease remains vested
    in the Landlord.

2. The Lease contains the following covenants on the part of the
    Tenant thereunder:

    "4.10.1:   Not to use the Demised Premises or permit or suffer
    them to be used otherwise than for the retail sale of sports goods."

    "4.15.1:   Not without the landlord's prior written consent in
    writing to assign this Lease or sub-let the Demised Premises in
    whole or in part and not to part with or share possession or occu-
    pation of the Demised Premises in whole or in part"

---

1   The notice is addressed to both Mitchell and Fowler because it is possible that the
    lease has been assigned. It is a registrable lease, so that the position can be checked
    by a Land Registry search. However, if Mitchell still appears as registered pro-
    prietor that does not exclude the possibility of an assignment, since it may be that
    the substitution of Fowler as registered proprietor has been applied for but has yet
    to be completed. To guard against the possibility of a change in proprietor being
    registered after posting but before service is effected, it is prudent to address the
    notice to both of them.

2   This and numbered paragraph 1 simply establish who is who, and the landlord's
    entitlement to serve the notice.

3. In breach of covenant 4.10.1 the Demised Premises are being used for the retail sale of flowers.

4. In breach of covenant 4.15.1 the Tenant has, without the Landlord's prior written consent:[3]

   a. assigned the Lease to the Occupier for the residue of the term thereof; alternatively

   b. sub-let the Demised Premises to the Occupier; alternatively

   c. parted with possession or occupation of the Demised Premises to the Occupier; alternatively

   d. shared possession or occupation of the Demised Premises with the Occupier.

---

3 The landlord cannot know yet precisely what arrangement exists between Mitchell and Fowler. Unless the breach of covenant is accurately identified in the notice any purported forfeiture will be unlawful, so it is necessary to cover all the bases by drafting in the alternative. This is often the case in relation to breaches of alien-ation covenant.

5. You are hereby required to remedy those breaches of covenant[4], insofar as they are capable of remedy, within a reasonable time[5] of the date of service of this Notice upon you.

6. You are hereby further required to compensate the Landlord in money for those breaches of covenant.[6]

7. Take notice that in the event that you fail to comply with this Notice the Landlord intends to forfeit the Lease, upon which you will cease to have any further interest in the Demised Premises and will lose the right to possession thereof.

Please sign and return the enclosed duplicate of this Notice by way of acknowledging safe receipt.

<u>Signed for and on behalf of the Landlord</u>

Dated 22 October 2019

---

4 The notice makes no reference to the arrears of rent, since forfeiture in reliance on arrears of rent does not require a s.146 notice.

5 Remedying the breach of user covenant, in this case, can be done by crossing the floor and putting the 'closed' sign up on the door, and so a reasonable time will be very short. As regards the alienation breach, an assignment or sub-letting without landlord's consent is regarded as irremediable, so again the reasonable time will be extremely short – however, the tenant should still be given a short period to consider its options and take advice. The alienation breach may, however, be a parting with or sharing of possession or occupation, which may not be considered irremediable, in which case there is a necessarily uncertain assessment to be made as to how long it might take Mitchell to remove Fowler from the premises. In light of the uncertainty, it is safest to stipulate for remedy of the breach within a reasonable time without attempting to put a date on it. That leaves the landlord to assess what the reasonable time may be in the light of events as they develop.

6 This is an optional requirement, and has been included for illustrative purposes. For this kind of breach, it is unlikely that the landlord will be seeking monetary compensation.

Example Particulars Of Claim[7]

(Claim issued 21 December 2019)[8]

1. By a lease ("the Lease") dated 24 April 2017 and made between Beale Investments Ltd ("the Claimant") and Phillip Mitchell ("the First Defendant"), premises known as 6 Albert Square, Walford, London E20 ("the Demised Premises") were let to the First Defendant for a term of ten years from the date of the Lease at the annual rent of £15,000 up to 23 April 2022, and thereafter at a rental to be determined upon review.

2. The Demised Premises are not residential, being let for use as a retail shop.[9]

3. The Claimant remains entitled to the reversion immediately expectant upon expiry of the Lease.

4. The Lease contains the following covenants on the tenant's part:

   a. By clause 4.1 "To pay the Principal Rent by equal quarterly instalments in advance on the usual quarter days"

   b. By clause 4.3 "To pay interest on any sums due from the Tenant to the Landlord hereunder which are unpaid and outstanding for more than seven days after the due date for payment at the rate of 2% per annum.

---

7 The landlord has decided to proceed by way of court proceedings rather than by peaceable re-entry. We do not know the factors which have led to that decision.

8 The landlord has left almost two months from the date of the notice before issuing proceedings. This may well be a reasonable time, but that is a fact-dependent assessment in each case.

9 Practice Direction 55A requires that the Particulars identify whether the property is residential or not.

    c. By clause 4.10.1 "Not to use the Demised Premises or permit or suffer them to be used otherwise than for the retail sale of sports goods."

    d. By clause 4.15.1 "Not without the landlord's prior written consent in writing to assign this Lease or sub-let the Demised Premises in whole or in part and not to part with or share possession or occupation of the Demised Premises in whole or in part"

5. By clause 7.1 of the Lease it is provided that the Landlord should be entitled to forfeit the Lease in the event that the tenant should be in breach of any of the covenants on the tenant's part contained in the Lease.

6. A copy of the Lease is served with these Particulars of Claim, and the Claimant will refer to it at trial for its full meaning and effect.

7. The First Defendant has failed to pay the instalment of Principal Rent due under the Lease on 29 September 2019 in the amount of £3750.00.

8. Interest is due on the unpaid Principal Rent pursuant to clause 4.3 of the Lease, amounting to £17.05 at the date hereof, being 83 days after the due date for payment, and continuing to accrue at the rate of 2% per annum, being a daily rate of £0.21, until judgment or sooner payment.

Particulars

£3750 x 2% x 83/365 = £17.05

9. Upon visiting the Premises on 15 October 2019, Ian Beale of the Claimant company discovered that the Premises are wholly given over to a florist's business trading as Fowler's Flowers. He was informed by Katherine Slater, believed to be an assistant in the

florist's business, that the proprietor of the business is Martin Fowler ("the Second Defendant").

10. No consent has ever been sought from the Claimant to the occupation of the Premises by the Second Defendant.

11. The First Defendant has breached the terms of clause 4.10.1 of the Lease in that the premises are being used for the retail sale of flowers.

12. The First Defendant has moreover breached the terms of clause 4.15.1 of the Lease by:

    a. Assigning the Lease to the Second Defendant for the residue of the term thereof; alternatively

    b. Sub-letting the Premises to the Second Defendant; alternatively

    c. Parting with possession or occupation of the Premises to the Second Defendant; alternatively

    d. Sharing possession or occupation of the Premises with the Second Defendant.

13. Full particulars of the precise nature of the breach of clause 4.15.1 will be given following disclosure in these proceedings.

14. The Claimant caused a Notice under section 146 of the Law of Property Act 1925 to be served upon the First and Second Defendants by posting on 22 October 2019, specifying the breaches of covenant under clauses 4.10.1 and 4.15.1 of the Lease, and stating that if the said breaches were not remedied within a reasonable time of service of that notice it was the Claimant's intention to forfeit the Lease.

15. Notwithstanding service of that Notice, those breaches of covenant have not been remedied, and the use of the Premises by the Second

Defendant for the business of a florist is continuing at the date of issue of these proceedings.

16. The Claimant is entitled to possession of the Premises by virtue of clause 7.1 of the Lease, and by the issue and service of these proceedings the Lease is forfeited to the Claimant.

17. There is to the Claimant's knowledge no person in possession of the Premises other than the First and Second Defendants.[10]

18. There is to the Claimant's knowledge no person other than the First and Second Defendants who is entitled to claim relief against forfeiture of the Lease.[11]

AND THE CLAIMANT CLAIMS:

a) Possession of the Premises;

b) £3,750 arrears of Principal Rent;

c) Interest at the rate of 2% per annum pursuant to the Lease, from and including 30 September 2019, amounting to £17.05 at the date hereof and continuing to accrue at the daily rate of £0.21 until judgment or sooner payment

d) Mesne profits at the rate of £15,000 per annum (being a daily rate of £41.10) from 25 December 2019 until such time as possession is delivered up;

---

10 Required by Practice Direction 55A

11 Not required by Practice Direction 55A, since the premises are not residential, but it is useful to set this out for clarity, and may help in obtaining the declaration sought as to relief.

e) Interest on mesne profits pursuant to s.69 of the County Courts Act 1984 from the date of service herein until judgment or sooner payment;

f) A declaration that there shall be no grant of relief against forfeiture;

g) Costs; and

h) Further or other relief.

MORE BOOKS BY
LAW BRIEF PUBLISHING

A selection of our other titles available now:-

'Ellis on Credit Hire – Sixth Edition' by Aidan Ellis & Tim Kevan
'A Practical Guide to Coercive Control for Legal Practitioners and Victims' by Rachel Horman
'A Practical Guide to Rights Over Airspace and Subsoil' by Daniel Gatty
'Tackling Disclosure in the Criminal Courts – A Practitioner's Guide' by Narita Bahra QC & Don Ramble
'A Practical Guide to the Law of Driverless Cars – Second Edition' by Alex Glassbrook, Emma Northey & Scarlett Milligan
'A Practical Guide to TOLATA Claims' by Greg Williams
'Artificial Intelligence – The Practical Legal Issues' by John Buyers
'A Practical Guide to the Law of Bullying and Harassment in the Workplace' by Philip Hyland
'How to Be a Freelance Solicitor: A Practical Guide to the SRA-Regulated Freelance Solicitor Model' by Paul Bennett
'A Practical Guide to Prison Injury Claims' by Malcolm Johnson
'A Practical Guide to the Small Claims Track' by Dominic Bright
'A Practical Guide to Advising Clients at the Police Station' by Colin Stephen McKeown-Beaumont
'A Practical Guide to Antisocial Behaviour Injunctions' by Iain Wightwick
'Practical Mediation: A Guide for Mediators, Advocates, Advisers, Lawyers, and Students in Civil, Commercial, Business, Property, Workplace, and Employment Cases' by Jonathan Dingle with John Sephton
'The Mini-Pupillage Workbook' by David Boyle
'Planning Obligations Demystified: A Practical Guide to Planning Obligations and Section 106 Agreements' by Bob Mc Geady & Meyric Lewis
'A Practical Guide to Crofting Law' by Brian Inkster

These books and more are available to order online direct from the publisher at www.lawbriefpublishing.com, where you can also read free sample chapters. For any queries, contact us on 0844 587 2383 or mail@lawbriefpublishing.com.

Our books are also usually in stock at www.amazon.co.uk with free next day delivery for Prime members, and at good legal bookshops such as Wildy & Sons.

We are regularly launching new books in our series of practical day-to-day practitioners' guides. Visit our website and join our free newsletter to be kept informed and to receive special offers, free chapters, etc.

You can also follow us on Twitter at www.twitter.com/lawbriefpub.